PLASTIC CANVAS
Christmas™
Celebrations

Edited by Laura Scott

HOUSE of
WHITE
BIRCHES

PUBLISHERS
SINCE 1947

Editor: Laura Scott
Associate Editor: June Sprunger
Copy Editor: Cathy Reef

Photography: Tammy Christian, Nora Elsesser
Photography Assistant: Linda Quinlan

Production Manager: Vicki Macy
Creative Coordinator: Shaun Venish
Book Design/Production: Dan Kraner
Production Coordinator: Sandra Beres
Production Assistants: Cheryl Lynch, Darren Powell, Jessica Rothe, Miriam Zacharias

Publishers: Carl H. Muselman, Arthur K. Muselman
Chief Executive Officer: John Robinson
Marketing Director: Scott Moss
Editorial Director: Vivian Rothe
Production Director: Scott Smith

Printed in the United States of America
First Printing: 1996
Library of Congress Number: 96-77023
ISBN: 1-882138-21-X

Every effort has been made to ensure the accuracy and completeness of the
instructions in this book. However, we cannot be responsible for human
error or for the results when using materials other than those specified in
the instructions, or for variations in individual work.

Cover projects: Snowman Match Holder, page 41; Mr. & Mrs. Santa Bear, page 92;
Surprise Bear, page 22; and Beary Special Christmas, page 14.

Dear Friends,

Celebrate the Christmas season with all the joy and love your heart can hold! Reminisce with family and friends, and create wonderful new traditions your children will cherish. And, be sure to make plastic canvas crafting a part of your festivities!

This volume brings you dozens upon dozens of delightfully festive projects that you'll love to stitch and share with the special people in your life. Decorating for the holidays is a pleasure you can enjoy year-round as you carefully stitch projects that will deck your halls and trim your tree! Ornaments, mantel decorations, stockings, a special Christmas clock and more will whet your creative appetite.

Planning your gift-giving is another Christmas pastime that isn't limited to December. You can create beautiful, hand-stitched gifts for family, friends and co-workers that will be appreciated for years to come. Sparkling jewelry, pretty photo albums, beaded desk accessories, decorative cottages and many more exciting gifts are at your fingertips!

You'll find everything you need to make your Christmas an extra-special celebration complete with your personal, hand-stitched touch!

Happy Stitching & Celebrating!

Laura Scott

Contents

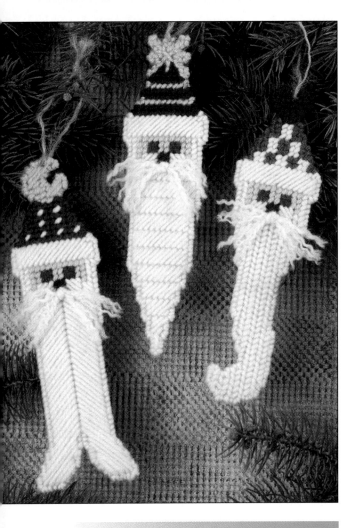

Decorating Your Holiday Home

Trimming the Tree

Treasured Gifts

The Christmas Kitchen

Stockings & Stocking Stuffers

Santa & Friends

Trimming the Tree

Give your Christmas tree a special look that is uniquely you by stitching beautiful, handmade ornaments! From a trio of charming, folk-art Santa ornaments to whimsical candy cane huggers, you'll find more than two dozen festive trims for your tree!

Candy Cane Huggers

Create this set of four colorful ornaments including Santa, a cheerful elf, a Christmas mouse and a cuddly teddy bear!

COLOR KEY

Plastic Canvas Yarn	Yards
☐ White #0001	14
☐ Peach #0007	1
☐ Cherry blossom #0010	1
☐ Curry #0014	3
☐ Taupe #0020	12
☐ Scarlet #0022	29
☐ Brisk green #0027	8
■ Black #0028	2
☐ Flesh #0033	2
☐ Silver grey #0045	9
☐ Walnut #0047	1
☐ Almond #0056	1
⁄ White #0001 Backstitch and Straight Stitch	
⁄ Scarlet #0022 Backstitch	
● Attach 4mm blue bead	
— Attach black oval cabochon	
◔ Attach 4mm black cabochon	
● Attach 5mm black cabochon	

Color numbers given are for Spinrite plastic canvas yarn.

Elf Leg
12 holes x 16 holes
Cut 2, reverse 1

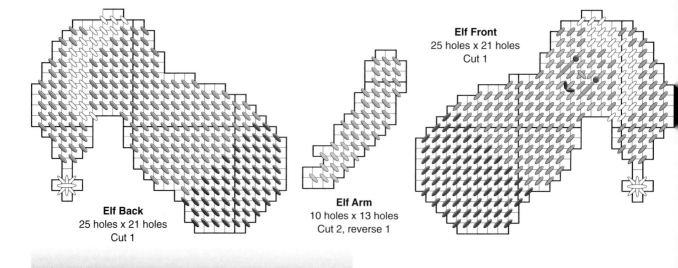

Elf Back
25 holes x 21 holes
Cut 1

Elf Arm
10 holes x 13 holes
Cut 2, reverse 1

Elf Front
25 holes x 21 holes
Cut 1

8

Skill Level: Intermediate

Materials

- 2½ sheets 7-count plastic canvas
- Plastic canvas yarn as listed in color key
- 3 (5mm) black round cabochons
- 2 (4mm) black round cabochons
- 6mm x 4mm black oval cabochon
- 4 (4mm) blue beads
- 24" fine gold braid
- Monofilament line
- Low-temperature glue gun

Instructions

1. Cut plastic canvas according to graphs (pages 8–10).

2. Stitch pieces following graphs, reversing four candy canes and one arm and one leg each for Santa, elf, bear and mouse.

3. Work all Backstitches over completed Continental Stitches using 2 plies scarlet for mouth of elf, mouse and bear and 2 plies white for mouse's hat and sweater.

4. Matching edges, Whipstitch wrong sides of two candy canes together with adjacent colors. Repeat with remaining candy canes.

5. For eyes on Santa and elf, attach beads with monofilament line where indicated on graph.

6. With wrong sides together, Whipstitch Santa front and back together with adjacent colors; elf front and back together with adjacent colors, using flesh on face areas; bear front and back together with taupe, using adjacent colors for scarf areas; and mouse front and back together with gray, using scarlet for sweater areas and hat top.

7. Glue 5mm cabochons on bear for eyes and nose where indicated on graph. For mouse, glue on 4mm cabochons for eyes and oval cabochon for nose where indicated on graph.

8. Overcast edges of all arms and legs with adjacent colors. Using photo as a guide, glue one arm and one leg on each side of corresponding character; glue hands and feet to candy canes.

9. Cut gold braid into four 6" pieces. Thread braid through center top of each character (not candy canes); tie ends in a knot.

—Designed by Darla Fanton

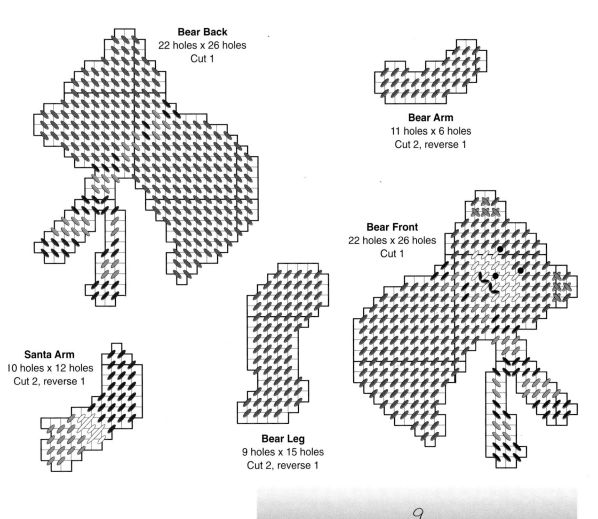

Bear Back
22 holes x 26 holes
Cut 1

Bear Arm
11 holes x 6 holes
Cut 2, reverse 1

Bear Front
22 holes x 26 holes
Cut 1

Santa Arm
10 holes x 12 holes
Cut 2, reverse 1

Bear Leg
9 holes x 15 holes
Cut 2, reverse 1

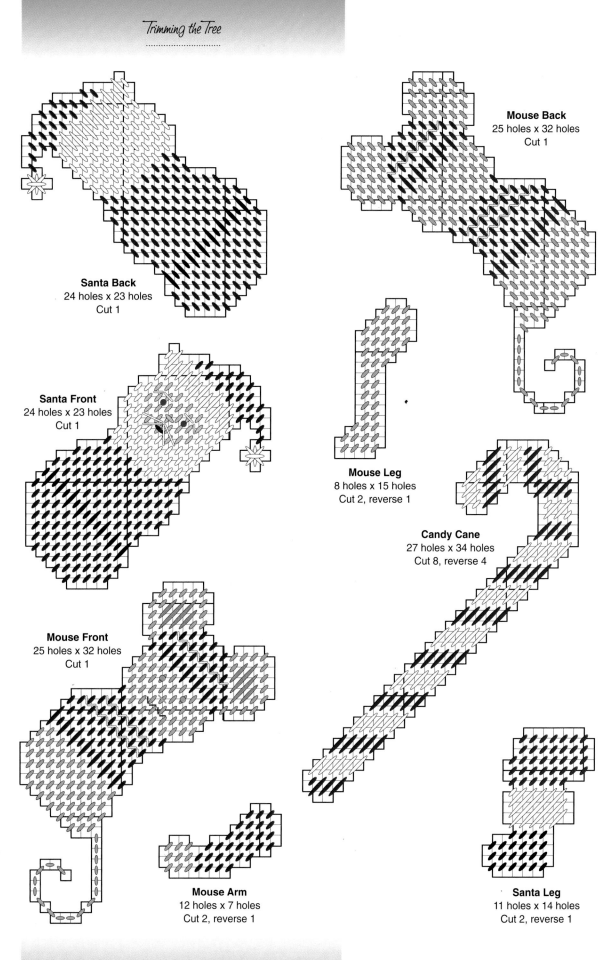

Santa Back
24 holes x 23 holes
Cut 1

Mouse Back
25 holes x 32 holes
Cut 1

Santa Front
24 holes x 23 holes
Cut 1

Mouse Leg
8 holes x 15 holes
Cut 2, reverse 1

Candy Cane
27 holes x 34 holes
Cut 8, reverse 4

Mouse Front
25 holes x 32 holes
Cut 1

Mouse Arm
12 holes x 7 holes
Cut 2, reverse 1

Santa Leg
11 holes x 14 holes
Cut 2, reverse 1

Each of these rustic Santa ornaments has its own unique stitching style and charm!

Skill Level: Beginner

Materials

- 1¼ sheets 7-count plastic canvas
- Plastic canvas yarn as listed in color key
- 3-ply jute
- Hot-glue gun

Instructions

1. Cut and stitch plastic canvas according to graphs (below and page 13).

2. Whipstitch wrong sides of fronts and backs together as follows: Santa A, Whipstitch hat areas together with paddy green and remaining edges together with adjacent colors; Santa B, Whipstitch together with adjacent colors; Santa C, Whipstitch hat areas together with Windsor blue and remaining edges together with adjacent colors.

3. For each mustache, cut two

4" lengths of natural yarn. Holding two lengths together, tie an overhand knot in center; fray ends. Glue knot under nose.

4. For hangers, cut a 9" length of jute and separate strands. Thread one strand each through holes indicated on graphs. Tie ends in a knot.

—Designed by Nancy Marshall

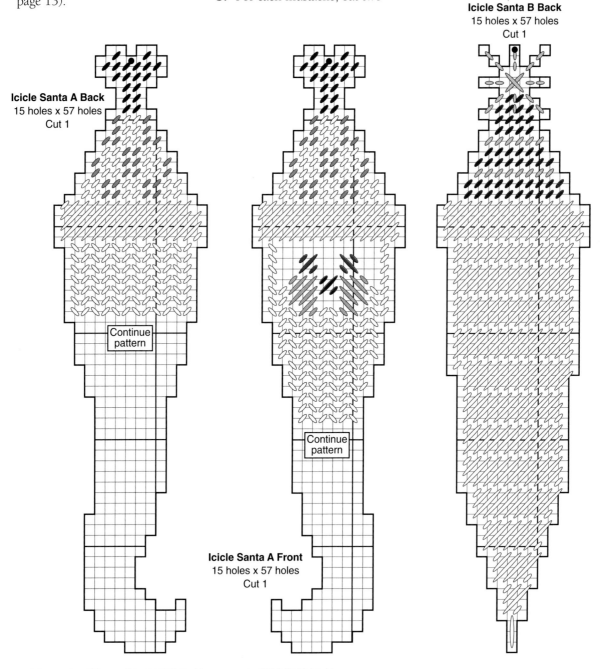

Icicle Santa A Back
15 holes x 57 holes
Cut 1

Continue pattern

Icicle Santa A Front
15 holes x 57 holes
Cut 1

Continue pattern

Icicle Santa B Back
15 holes x 57 holes
Cut 1

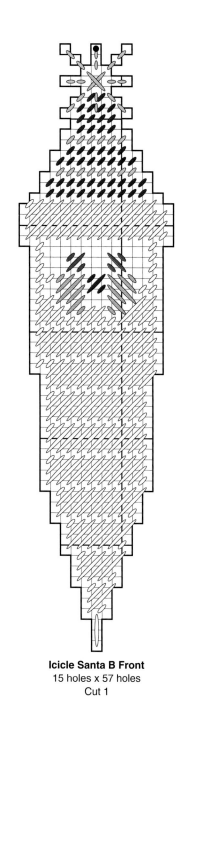

Icicle Santa B Front
15 holes x 57 holes
Cut 1

COLOR KEY

Plastic Canvas Yarn	Yards
☐ Natural #111	35
▨ Honey gold #645	3½
▨ Paddy green #686	1¼
▨ Lily pink #719	1½
▨ Windsor blue #808	3½
■ Cardinal #917	3½
Uncoded areas are flesh	
#248 Continental Stitches	1½
● Attach hanger	

Color numbers given are for J. & P.
Coats plastic canvas yarn.

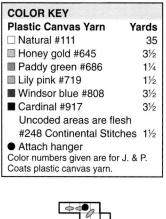

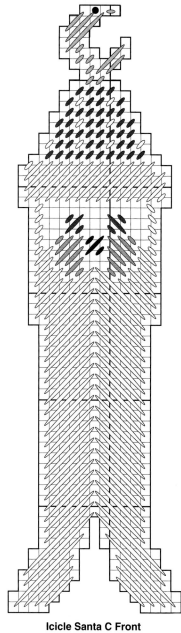

Icicle Santa C Front
17 holes x 57 holes
Cut 1

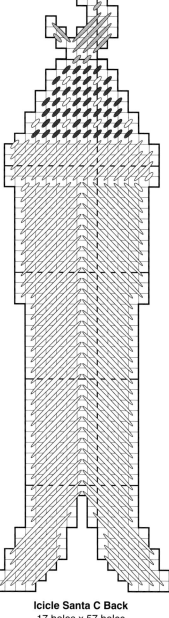

Icicle Santa C Back
17 holes x 57 holes
Cut 1

Beary
Special Christmas

These adorable ornaments are
super-quick to stitch and will delight
anyone with a soft spot for teddy bears.

Skill Level: Beginner

Christmas Gift Bear

Materials

- ¼ sheet soft 7-count plastic canvas
- Plastic canvas yarn as listed in color key
- #16 tapestry needle
- 1" white flocked bear
- 8" silver filament
- Hot-glue gun

Instructions

1. Cut plastic canvas according to graphs (lower right).

2. Stitch pieces following graphs. Overcast the four box top edges with holly and the four lid edges with adjacent colors. Whipstitch box and lid sides corners together with holly.

3. Thread filament where indicated on box lid; tie ends in a knot.

4. Using photo as a guide, glue bear into box diagonally, then glue lid on box and bear so bear is peeking out from under lid.

Sledding Santa Bear

Materials

- ¼ sheet stiff 7-count plastic canvas
- Plastic canvas yarn as listed in color key
- Metallic craft cord as listed in color key
- #16 tapestry needle
- 1½" brown flocked Santa bear
- Hot-glue gun

Instructions

1. Cut plastic canvas according to graphs (upper right).

2. Stitch pieces following graphs, reversing one sled runner before stitching. Overcast sled board with red and sled runners with black/gold.

3. Glue top edge of each runner to board sides, then center and glue Santa bear to board.

Sledding Reclining Bear

Materials

- ¼ sheet stiff 7-count plastic canvas
- Plastic canvas yarn as listed in color key
- Metallic craft cord as listed in color key
- #16 tapestry needle
- 1" white flocked half-bear
- 8" gold filament
- Hot-glue gun

Instructions

1. Cut plastic canvas according to graphs.

2. Stitch pieces following graphs, reversing one sled runner before stitching. Overcast sled board with gold and sled runners with black/gold.

3. Glue top edge of each runner to board sides, then center and glue Santa to board.

4. For hanger, thread gold filament through top center hole of sled board, tie ends in a knot.

— Designed by Angie Arickx

COLOR KEY	
Plastic Canvas Yarn	**Yards**
■ Red #01	10
☐ Gold #17	3
▨ Holly #27	6
☐ White #41	4
◯ Red #01 Turkey Loop	
Metallic Craft Cord	
■ Black/gold #93	6⅓
● Attach silver filament	
Color numbers given are for Uniek Needloft plastic canvas yarn and Mangelsen's metallic craft cord.	

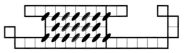

Santa Bear Sled Runner
17 holes x 4 holes
Cut 2, reverse 1

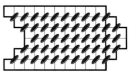

Santa Bear Sled Board
12 holes x 6 holes
Cut 1

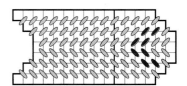

Reclining Bear Sled Board
16 holes x 7 holes
Cut 1

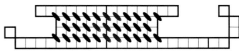

Reclining Bear Sled Runner
23 holes x 4 holes
Cut 2, reverse 1

Christmas Gift Box
18 holes x 18 holes
Cut 1

Christmas Gift Box Lid
11 holes x 11 holes
Cut 1

Angel Wings

Skill Level: Intermediate

Materials

- 14-count plastic canvas heart
- 6-strand embroidery floss as listed in color key
- ⅛" metallic ribbon as listed in color key
- #24 tapestry needle
- Set of 4" gold puffy angel wings
- Hot-glue gun

Instructions

1. Using entire length of cream floss, work diagonal stitches following graph (page 17). Work vertical rows of gold French Knots alternating with vertical rows of gold Continental Stitches as per graph.

2. With gold, stitch around heart from inside edge of outer band to connecting hole on heart shape. Overcast heart with cream.

3. For hanger, cut a 10" length of gold ribbon and glue ends to top backside of heart (see photo). **Note:** *Hanger may be omitted if using angel wings on tote bag, wreath, etc.*

4. Using photo as a guide, glue wings to center back of heart.

— *Designed by Joan Green*

Christmas Sparkle Ornaments

Skill Level: Intermediate

Materials

- ¼ sheet 14-count plastic canvas
- 6-strand embroidery floss as listed in color key
- ¹⁄₁₆" metallic ribbon as listed in color key
- #22 tapestry needle
- 2 (½") squares synthetic suede or felt
- Tacky glue

Project Note

When working with metallic ribbon, keep ribbon smooth and flat. To prevent twisting and tangling, guide ribbon between thumb and forefinger of free hand. Drop needle occasionally to let ribbon unwind.

Instructions

1. Cut two plastic canvas pieces according to graph (below).

2. Stitch one piece following graph. Overcast with ruby ribbon, stitching three times in outer corners for best coverage. Stitch remaining piece reversing colors, Overcasting with Vatican ribbon.

3. For each ornament, cut a 6" length of ribbon the same color as the Overcasting ribbon. Fold ribbon in half and sew or glue ends to center top of ornament.

4. Using ornaments as templates, cut synthetic suede or felt to fit backside. Spread a thin layer of glue on fabric and pat gently on back of ornament, making sure glue does not seep through. Allow to dry overnight.

— *Designed by Judi Kauffman*

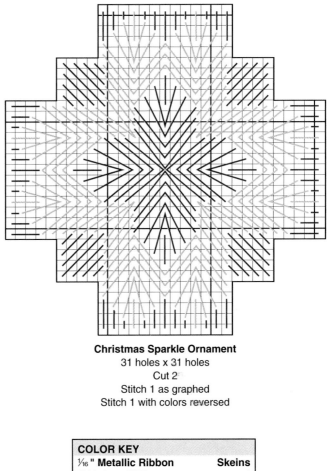

Christmas Sparkle Ornament
31 holes x 31 holes
Cut 2
Stitch 1 as graphed
Stitch 1 with colors reversed

COLOR KEY	
¹⁄₁₆" Metallic Ribbon	**Skeins**
▨ Vatican #102	1
Ruby #061 Overcasting	1
6-Strand Embroidery Floss	
▣ Shaded red #75	1
Color numbers given are for Kreinik ¹⁄₁₆" Ribbon and DMC 6-strand embroidery floss.	

Angel Wings & Christmas Sparkle Ornaments

Add a little sparkle to your Christmas tree with these three dazzling ornaments.

Angel Wings Heart
Stitch 1

COLOR KEY	
6-Strand Embroidery Floss	**Yards**
☐ Cream #712	3
⅛" Metallic Ribbon	
☐ Gold #202HL	3
⚪ Gold #202HL French Knot	
Color numbers given are for DMC 6-strand embroidery floss and Kreinik ⅛" Ribbon.	

Country Christmas Charm

Give your Christmas tree a rustic look with this set of four charming ornaments.

Skill Level: Beginner

Christmas Cat

Materials
- ½ sheet 7-count plastic canvas
- Plastic canvas yarn as listed in color key
- #3 pearl cotton as listed in color key
- 12" ¼"-wide green satin ribbon
- 12" white/gold metallic cord
- Small brass bell

Instructions
1. Cut plastic canvas according to graph (page 20).

2. Stitch pieces following graph, adding black French Knots and Backstitches to front piece only.

3. With wrong sides together, Whipstitch front to back with adjacent colors, using eggshell across shoulders.

4. Wrap green ribbon around cat's neck, thread bell onto ribbon and tie ribbon in a bow (see photo).

5. For hanger, thread metallic cord through holes indicated on graph; tie ends in a bow.

Stocking Mouse

Materials
- ⅔ sheet 7-count plastic canvas
- Plastic canvas yarn as listed in color key
- #3 pearl cotton as listed in color key
- 12" white/gold metallic cord

Instructions
1. Cut plastic canvas according to graphs (page 21).

2. Stitch pieces following graphs, adding black French Knots and Backstitches over completed Continental Stitches.

3. With wrong sides together, Whipstitch front to back with adjacent colors.

4. For hanger, thread metallic cord through holes indicated on graphs; tie ends in a bow.

Snowman

Materials
- ½ sheet 7-count plastic canvas
- Plastic canvas yarn as listed in color key
- #3 pearl cotton as listed in color key
- 12" white/gold metallic cord

Instructions
1. Cut plastic canvas according to graphs (see next page).

2. Stitch pieces following graphs, adding black French Knots and Backstitches over completed Continental Stitches.

3. With wrong sides together, Whipstitch front to back with adjacent colors, noting on graph where shoulders are Overcast with green; Whipstitch broom handles together with black.

4. For hanger, thread metallic cord through holes indicated on graphs; tie ends in a bow.

Little Christmas House

Materials
- ½ sheet 7-count plastic canvas
- Plastic canvas yarn as listed in color key
- Small ribbon and holly bouquet (sample bouquet included pinecone)
- Potpourri
- 12" gold metallic cord
- Hot-glue gun

Instructions
1. Cut plastic canvas according to graphs (see next page).

2. Stitch pieces following graphs. With Christmas red, Whipstitch house front, back and sides together, then Whipstitch base to assembled house.

3. With forest, Overcast side and bottom edges of roof pieces, then Whipstitch top edges together.

4. For hanger, thread metallic cord through holes indicated on graphs; tie ends in a bow. Attach ribbon and holly bouquet to hanger at roof peak.

5. Fill house with potpourri, then glue roof to house.

— Designed by Michele Wilcox

COLOR KEY	
LITTLE CHRISTMAS HOUSE	
Plastic Canvas Yarn	**Yards**
■ Christmas red #02	13
□ Tangerine #11	4
▨ Holly #27	1
■ Forest #29	7
● Attach hanger	
Color numbers given are for Uniek Needloft plastic canvas yarn.	

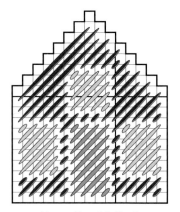

House Front & Back
15 holes x 18 holes
Cut 2

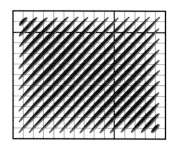

House Base
15 holes x 12 holes
Cut 1

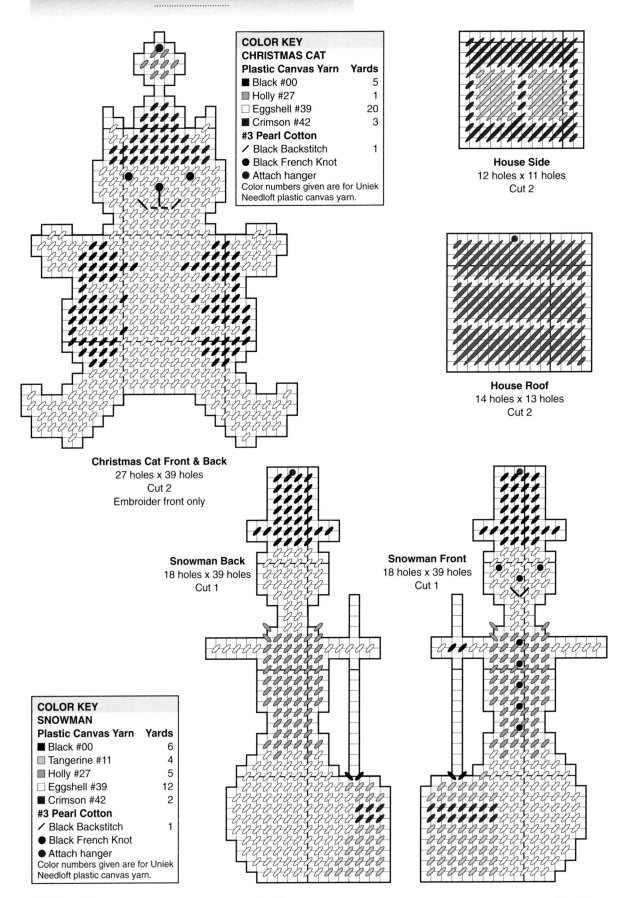

COLOR KEY
CHRISTMAS CAT

Plastic Canvas Yarn	Yards
■ Black #00	5
■ Holly #27	1
□ Eggshell #39	20
■ Crimson #42	3

#3 Pearl Cotton

╱ Black Backstitch	1
● Black French Knot	
● Attach hanger	

Color numbers given are for Uniek Needloft plastic canvas yarn.

House Side
12 holes x 11 holes
Cut 2

House Roof
14 holes x 13 holes
Cut 2

Christmas Cat Front & Back
27 holes x 39 holes
Cut 2
Embroider front only

Snowman Back
18 holes x 39 holes
Cut 1

Snowman Front
18 holes x 39 holes
Cut 1

COLOR KEY
SNOWMAN

Plastic Canvas Yarn	Yards
■ Black #00	6
□ Tangerine #11	4
■ Holly #27	5
□ Eggshell #39	12
■ Crimson #42	2

#3 Pearl Cotton

╱ Black Backstitch	1
● Black French Knot	
● Attach hanger	

Color numbers given are for Uniek Needloft plastic canvas yarn.

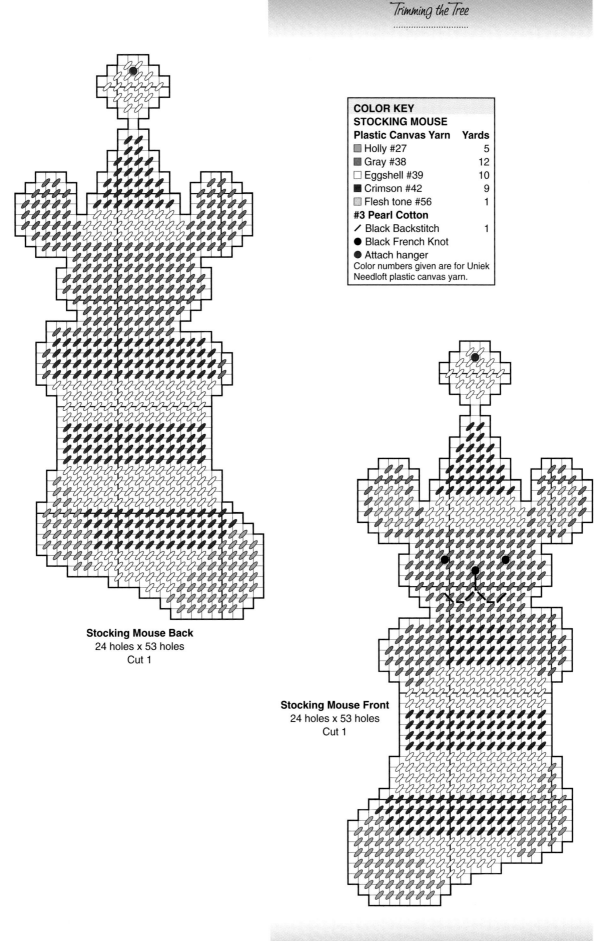

COLOR KEY
STOCKING MOUSE

Plastic Canvas Yarn	Yards
▨ Holly #27	5
▨ Gray #38	12
☐ Eggshell #39	10
■ Crimson #42	9
▨ Flesh tone #56	1
#3 Pearl Cotton	
╱ Black Backstitch	1
● Black French Knot	
● Attach hanger	

Color numbers given are for Uniek
Needloft plastic canvas yarn.

Stocking Mouse Back
24 holes x 53 holes
Cut 1

Stocking Mouse Front
24 holes x 53 holes
Cut 1

Surprise Bear

Stitch this whimsical jack-in-the-box bear as a special gift ornament!

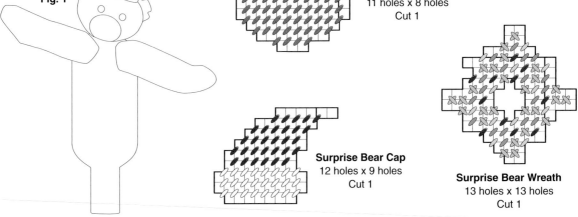

Fig. 1

Surprise Bear Head
11 holes x 8 holes
Cut 1

Surprise Bear Cap
12 holes x 9 holes
Cut 1

Surprise Bear Wreath
13 holes x 13 holes
Cut 1

Skill Level: Intermediate

Materials

- 1 sheet 10-count plastic canvas
- #3 pearl cotton as listed in color key
- Single-ply angora yarn as listed in color key
- 2 (4mm) movable eyes
- 6mm gold jingle bell
- 12" ⅛"-wide red double-faced satin ribbon
- ¼ sheet green tissue paper
- Hot-glue gun

Instructions

1. Cut plastic canvas according to graphs.

2. Stitch pieces following graphs, reversing one arm before stitching.

3. Overcast body, head, arms and ears with light tan brown and muzzle with adjacent color. Backstitch muzzle and arms with very dark mocha brown.

4. Overcast inside and outside edges of wreath with very dark emerald green and Santa cap with adjacent colors.

5. Using Christmas red throughout, Overcast top edges of three box sides. With wrong sides together, Whipstitch lid top and lid bottom together along side and top edges. Whipstitch box sides together and then box bottom to sides. Whipstitch bottom edges of lid to remaining top edge of box side so that lid bottom faces front.

6. Following photo and Fig. 1, glue ears to back of head; glue hat, muzzle and eyes to head front. Glue arms and head to upper body front. Glue bell to point of hat.

7. Thread 4½" red ribbon through top of wreath on back-side, centering wreath in middle

of ribbon. Glue ribbon ends to bear paws, trimming ends as needed before gluing.

8. Cut remaining ribbon in half and tie each in a small bow. Glue one bow to each paw. Trim ends of bow as desired.

9. Glue right side of bear to wrong side of box front. Stuff box with tissue paper.

— Designed by Celia Lange Designs

COLOR KEY

#3 Pearl Cotton	Yards
■ Christmas red #321	9
■ Light tan brown #437	7
☐ Ultra very light tan #739	3
■ Very dark emerald green #909	5
■ Medium Nile green #913	4
☐ Christmas gold #972	4
Uncoded areas are off-white #746 Continental Stitches	17
╱ Very dark mocha brown #838 Backstitch	1
Single-Ply Angora	
☐ White #SB 1	1

Color numbers given are for DMC #3 pearl cotton and Rainbow Gallery Santa's Beard & Suit.

Surprise Bear Ear
4 holes x 3 holes
Cut 2

Surprise Bear Muzzle
5 holes x 4 holes
Cut 1

Bear Arm
9 holes x 16 holes
Cut 2, reverse 1

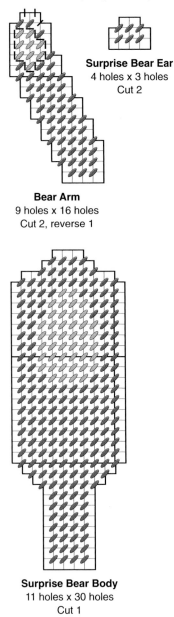

Surprise Bear Body
11 holes x 30 holes
Cut 1

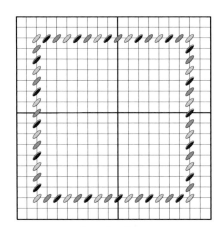

**Surprise Bear
Box Bottom & Lid Bottom**
19 holes x 19 holes
Cut 2

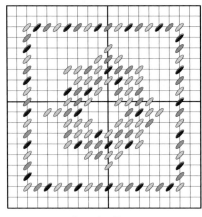

**Surprise Bear
Box Side & Lid Top**
19 holes x 19 holes
Cut 5

Festive Jinglers

Not only will these easy-to-stitch ornaments catch your eye, but they'll please your ears too with their jingle bell tummies!

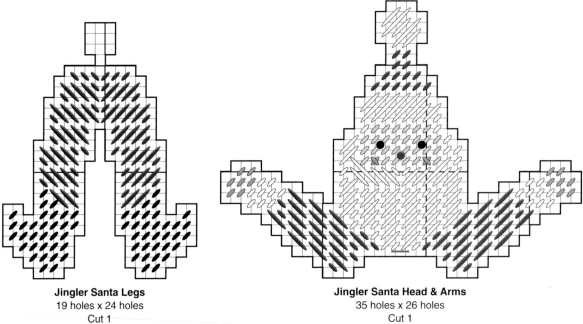

Jingler Santa Legs
19 holes x 24 holes
Cut 1

Jingler Santa Head & Arms
35 holes x 26 holes
Cut 1

Skill Level: Beginner

Materials

- ⅔ sheet 7-count plastic canvas
- Plastic canvas yarn as listed in color key
- #16 tapestry needle
- 2 (35mm) gold jingle bells
- Hot-glue gun

Instructions

1. Cut plastic canvas according to graphs.

2. Stitch Santa following graphs, Overcasting edges with adjacent colors while stitching; Overcast tab on upper edge of Santa legs with scarlet.

3. Stitch elf following graphs. Overcast edges while stitching as follows: elf legs with adjacent colors and tab with brisk green; elf ears with peach, arms and shoulders with brisk green and remaining edges with adjacent colors.

4. Add brisk green Straight Stitches over completed background stitching; Backstitch mouth on elf with 2 plies black yarn.

5. Add black French Knots for eyes, using 2 plies for elf only. For Santa's French Knot nose and elf's French Knot at center of bow, wrap yarn around needle twice.

6. Use brisk green to attach bell to elf and white to attach bell to Santa where indicated on graphs. Insert tab of leg sections into bottom slot of bell.

7. For hanger, cut an 8" length of white yarn for Santa, fold yarn in half and glue ends to top center back of pompon on hat. For elf, cut an 8" length of brisk green, fold yarn in half and glue ends to top center back of hat.

— Designed by Joan Green

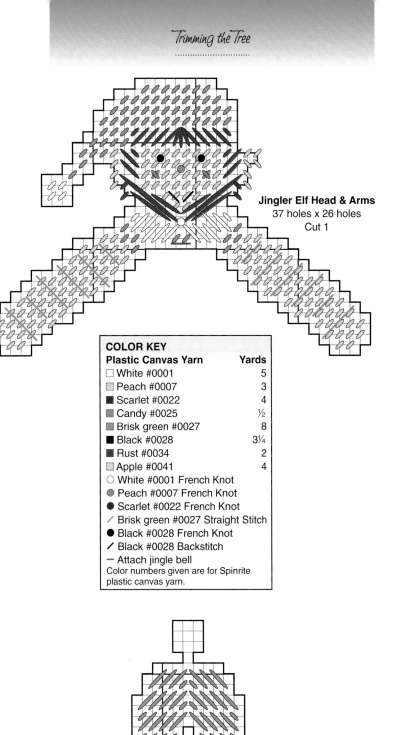

Jingler Elf Head & Arms
37 holes x 26 holes
Cut 1

COLOR KEY

Plastic Canvas Yarn	Yards
☐ White #0001	5
☐ Peach #0007	3
■ Scarlet #0022	4
▨ Candy #0025	½
▨ Brisk green #0027	8
■ Black #0028	3¼
■ Rust #0034	2
☐ Apple #0041	4
○ White #0001 French Knot	
● Peach #0007 French Knot	
● Scarlet #0022 French Knot	
╱ Brisk green #0027 Straight Stitch	
● Black #0028 French Knot	
╱ Black #0028 Backstitch	
— Attach jingle bell	

Color numbers given are for Spinrite plastic canvas yarn.

Jingler Elf Legs
25 holes x 25 holes
Cut 1

Noel Quartet

*Be sure to hang these pretty
ornaments together to share your
holiday spirit with your family!*

Skill Level: Beginner

Materials

- 1 sheet 7-count plastic canvas
- 4-ply acrylic craft yarn as listed in color key
- #16 tapestry needle
- Ceramic buttons: gingerbread man and woman, snowman, penguin, sled
- Sewing needle and thread
- 9" x 12" piece white felt
- Seam sealant
- Craft glue

Instructions

1. Cut plastic canvas pieces according to graphs.

2. Stitch pieces following graphs. Overcast the N with paddy green, the E with white and the O and the L with cherry pink.

3. Cut one 10" length each of cherry pink and paddy green; cut two 10" lengths of white. Thread yarn through center top hole of each ornament, using white with N and E, cherry pink with O and paddy green with L. Tie ends in a knot, allowing ¾" yarn above knots. Apply seam sealant to ends. Allow to dry.

4. Using photo as a guide, sew buttons above letters on ornaments as follows; snowman on the N, penguin on the O, sled on the E and gingerbread man and woman on the L.

5. Using ornaments as templates, cut felt to fit backsides; glue in place.

— Designed by Judi Kauffman

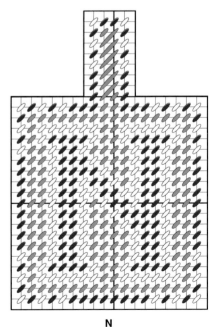

N
19 holes x 28 holes
Cut 1

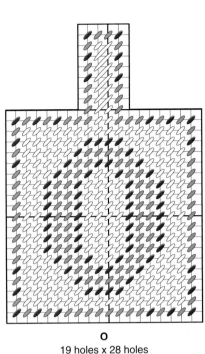

O
19 holes x 28 holes
Cut 1

COLOR KEY

4-Ply Craft Yarn	Yards
☐ White #1	12
▦ Paddy green #686	11
◼ Cherry pink #746	16

Color numbers given are for J. & P. Coats Art. E.48 acrylic craft yarn.

Grandma's Favorite Gingerbread Cookies

Ingredients

- ¼ cup butter
- ½ cup white or brown sugar
- ½ cup dark molasses
- 3½ cups sifted flour
- 1 teaspoon baking soda
- ¼ teaspoon cloves
- ½ teaspoon cinnamon
- 2 teaspoons ginger
- ½ teaspoon salt
- Gingerbread man cookie cutter

Instructions

Preheat oven to 350 degrees. Blend butter and sugar until creamy. Beat in molasses. In a separate bowl, sift flour, baking soda, cloves, cinnamon, ginger and salt together. Add sifted ingredients to butter-and-sugar mixture in 3 parts alternately with ¼ cup water.

Roll batter onto a large, greased cookie sheet. With cookie cutter, cut gingerbread man shapes. Peel away scraps of dough between gingerbread men and use to make more men.

Bake for 8 minutes or until dough springs back after pressing with finger. After cookies are cool, decorate with colored frosting to add clothing and features. Yields 16 thin gingerbread men.

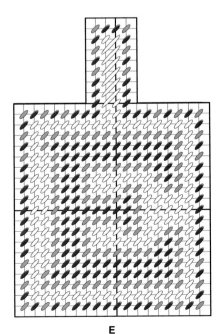

E
19 holes x 28 holes
Cut 1

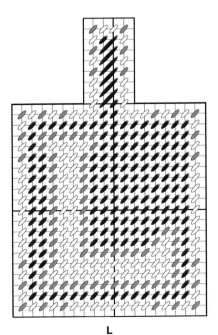

L
19 holes x 28 holes
Cut 1

Decorating Your Holiday Home

Give your house a special, Christmas touch by accenting it with festive, hand-stitched home decor. A gingerbread house, snowmen, nutcrackers, Christmas trees and other delightful designs will bring holiday warmth into every room in your home!

Gingerbread House
Not only does this clever decoration
display your treasured photos, but it also
doubles as a handy tissue box cover!

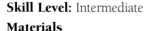

Skill Level: Intermediate

Materials
- 1½ sheets 7-count plastic canvas
- Plastic canvas yarn as listed in color key
- #16 tapestry needle
- Wreath button #86150
- Holly heart button #86015
- Sewing needle and thread
- Lightweight cardboard

Instructions

1. Cut plastic canvas according to graphs below and on next page.

2. Stitch pieces following graphs. Stitch French Knots over completed background stitching on chimney pieces. Overcast photo openings with brisk green.

3. With sewing needle and thread, sew wreath button to upper front door and heart button centered above photo cutout on front piece.

4. Cut cardboard to fit backside of front and side pieces. Trace around holes for photo placement.

5. Using antique gold throughout, Overcast side and bottom edges of roof pieces and bottom and top edges of box front, back and sides. Whipstitch sides to front and back.

6. Using white throughout, Overcast top edges of chimney pieces, then Whipstitch side edges together, alternating large and small pieces. Whipstitch top edges of roof pieces together on both sides of cutout. Whipstitch chimney to opening in roof.

7. Trim photos to fit in photo openings and glue to cardboard. Glue cardboard in place.

8. With antique gold, tack roof to house at several points along front and back pieces.

9. Insert tissue box, bringing tissue through chimney.

— *Designed by Joan Green*

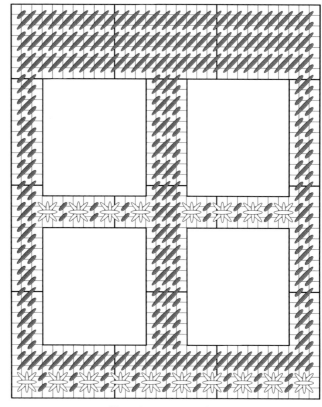

Gingerbread House Side
30 holes x 37 holes
Cut 2

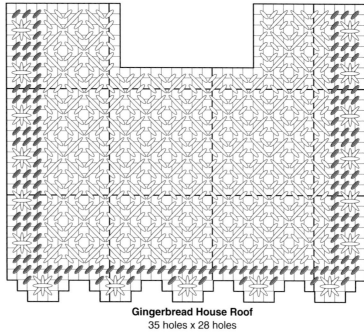

Gingerbread House Roof
35 holes x 28 holes
Cut 2

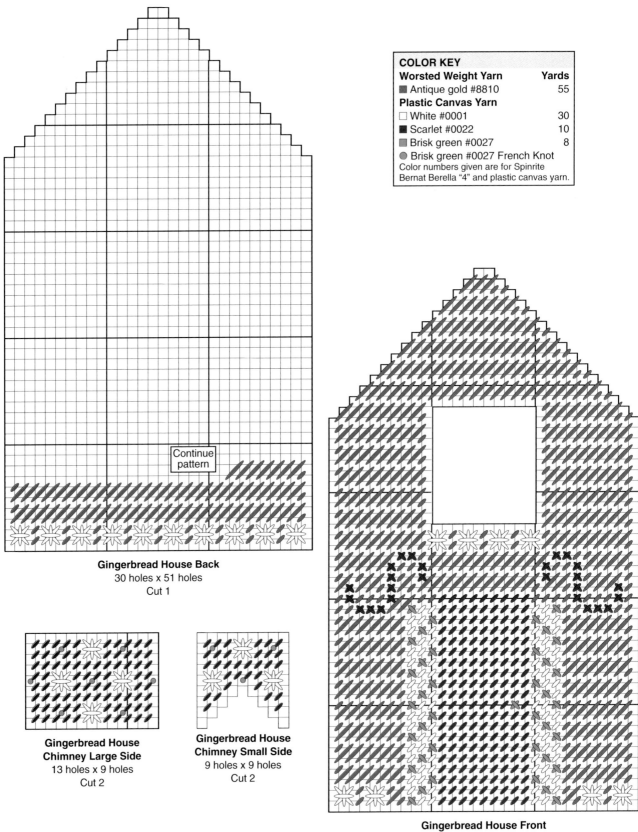

COLOR KEY

Worsted Weight Yarn	Yards
■ Antique gold #8810	55
Plastic Canvas Yarn	
□ White #0001	30
■ Scarlet #0022	10
■ Brisk green #0027	8
● Brisk green #0027 French Knot	

Color numbers given are for Spinrite
Bernat Berella "4" and plastic canvas yarn.

Gingerbread House Back
30 holes x 51 holes
Cut 1

**Gingerbread House
Chimney Large Side**
13 holes x 9 holes
Cut 2

**Gingerbread House
Chimney Small Side**
9 holes x 9 holes
Cut 2

Continue
pattern

Gingerbread House Front
30 holes x 51 holes
Cut 1

Collectors of miniatures can create their own special Christmas display on this unique tree design.

Skill Level: Advanced beginner

Materials
- 2 sheets 7-count stiff plastic canvas
- 2 (6") radial circles
- Plastic canvas yarn as listed in color key
- Straw satin raffia as listed in color key
- ¹⁄₁₆"-wide metallic ribbon as listed in color key
- Lighweight miniatures as desired (for shelves)
- Miniature toys and gift packages as desired (for base)
- Sawtooth hanger
- High-temperature glue gun

Cutting & Stitching

1. Cut canvas according to graphs (pages 34–36). Cut circles in half along straight center bars. **Note:** *The two half-circles with the straight center bars will be used. The remaining two half-circles will*

not be used in this project.

2. Stitch pieces following graphs, working embroidery over completed background stitching; embroider tree front only. Brace/back and shelf backs will remain unstitched. Overcast treetop star with gold.

3. Using white satin raffia on one half-circle for base bottom and red on remaining half-circle for base top, Straight Stitch each half-circle from the first outside row of holes to the fifth row of holes, using two stitches per hole as necessary in the fifth row of holes.

4. Moving toward the center or straight bar, repeat step 3, stitching pattern four more times from the fifth row of holes to the ninth, from the ninth to the 13th, from the 13th to the 17th and from the 17th to the two center holes.

5. With gold, Backstitch between each row of stitches on base top only.

Assembly

1. With white, Whipstitch bottom edge of base front to base bottom; Whipstitch base top to top edge of base front with gold.

2. With wrong sides together and using brisk green, Whipstitch together branches and top edges of tree front and back. Do not stitch bottom edges together.

3. Slip brace/back inside bottom of tree. With brisk green, Whipstitch bottom edges of tree to brace/back through all three layers where indicated on graph.

4. With red, Whipstitch back edge of base top to brace/back where indicated on graph. Whipstitch bottom edge of brace/back to base bottom with white. Whipstitch brace/back sides to base front sides using adjacent colors.

5. With clover, Whipstitch corresponding shelf fronts, backs and sides together, then Whipstitch shelf tops and bottoms to fronts, backs and sides.

6. Center and glue shelf backs to tree front where indicated on graph, beginning with smallest shelf at top, graduating to largest shelf at bottom.

7. Using photo as a guide, glue star to treetop, gift packages and toys to base and lightweight miniatures to shelves.

8. Glue or stitch sawtooth hanger to top back of tree.

— Designed by Celia Lange Designs

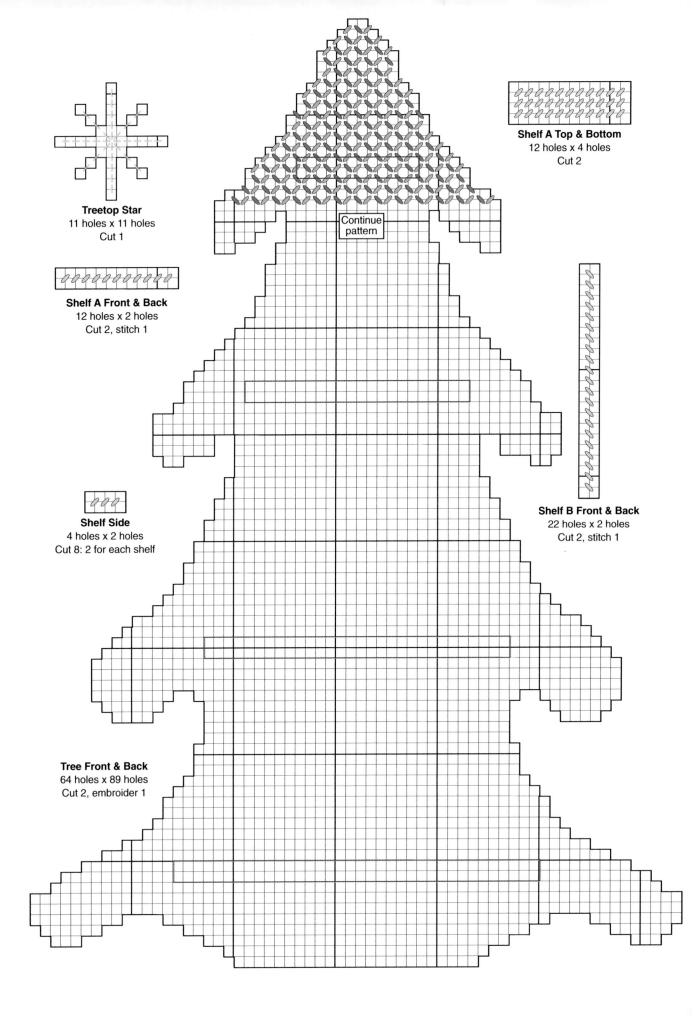

Treetop Star
11 holes x 11 holes
Cut 1

Shelf A Front & Back
12 holes x 2 holes
Cut 2, stitch 1

Shelf Side
4 holes x 2 holes
Cut 8: 2 for each shelf

Tree Front & Back
64 holes x 89 holes
Cut 2, embroider 1

Continue pattern

Shelf A Top & Bottom
12 holes x 4 holes
Cut 2

Shelf B Front & Back
22 holes x 2 holes
Cut 2, stitch 1

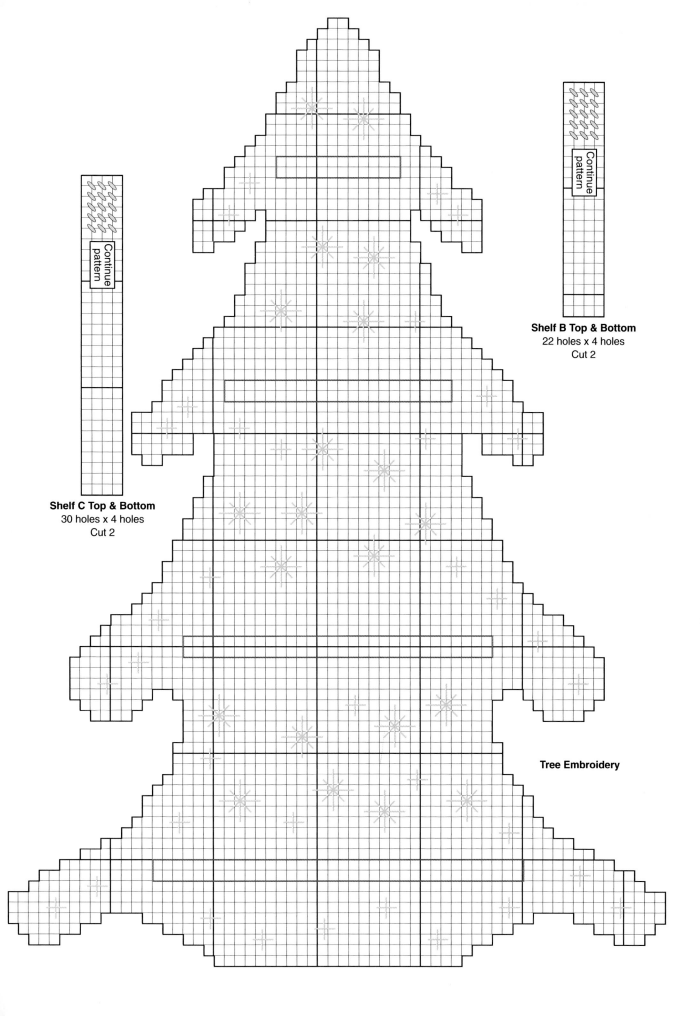

Shelf B Top & Bottom
22 holes x 4 holes
Cut 2

Continue pattern

Shelf C Top & Bottom
30 holes x 4 holes
Cut 2

Continue pattern

Tree Embroidery

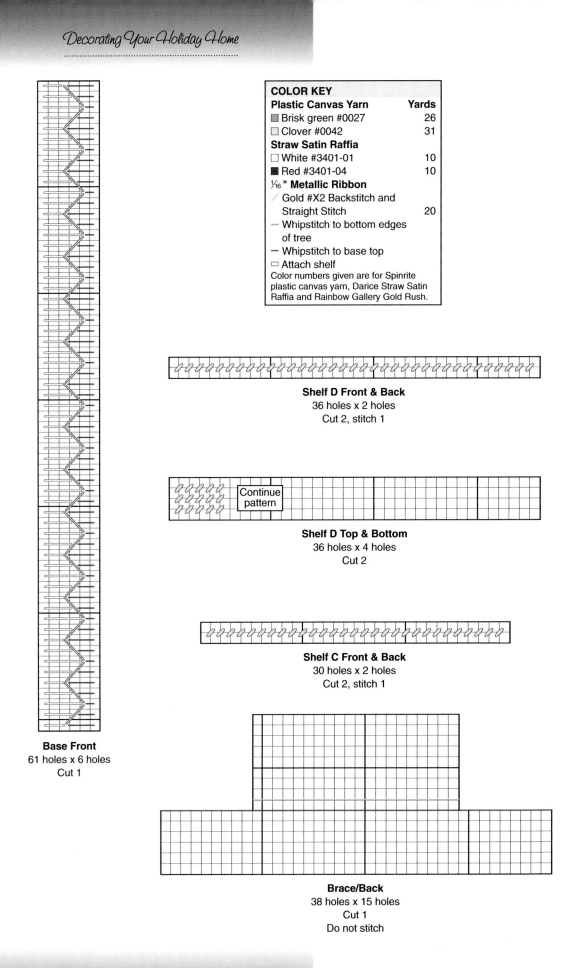

COLOR KEY

Plastic Canvas Yarn	Yards
▩ Brisk green #0027	26
☐ Clover #0042	31
Straw Satin Raffia	
☐ White #3401-01	10
■ Red #3401-04	10
¹⁄₁₆ " Metallic Ribbon	
╱ Gold #X2 Backstitch and Straight Stitch	20
— Whipstitch to bottom edges of tree	
— Whipstitch to base top	
▱ Attach shelf	

Color numbers given are for Spinrite plastic canvas yarn, Darice Straw Satin Raffia and Rainbow Gallery Gold Rush.

Base Front
61 holes x 6 holes
Cut 1

Shelf D Front & Back
36 holes x 2 holes
Cut 2, stitch 1

Continue pattern

Shelf D Top & Bottom
36 holes x 4 holes
Cut 2

Shelf C Front & Back
30 holes x 2 holes
Cut 2, stitch 1

Brace/Back
38 holes x 15 holes
Cut 1
Do not stitch

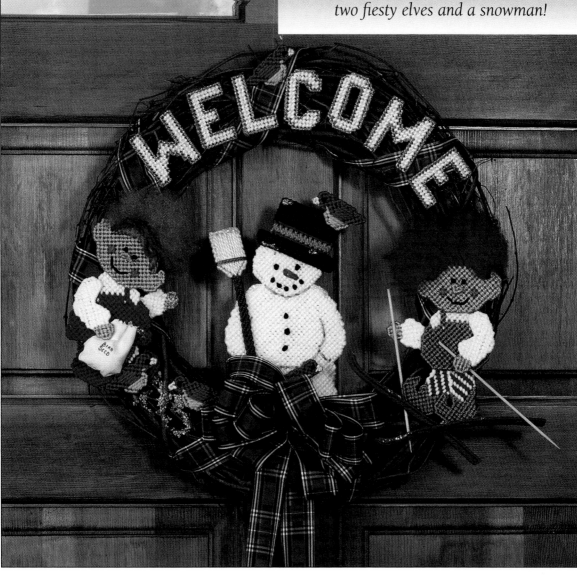

A Winter Welcome

*Give your home a whimsical touch
with this delightful wreath featuring
two fiesty elves and a snowman!*

Skill Level: Intermediate

Materials
- 1½ artist-size sheets 7-count plastic canvas
- Plastic canvas yarn as listed in color key
- Pearlized metallic cord as listed in color key
- Bright metallic cord as listed in color key
- 6 yards metallic cord: blue/silver #34021-115
- 18" grapevine wreath
- 5 yards 1⅜"-wide Scotch plaid ribbon

- 2½" x 3¾" piece muslin
- Extra-fine-point black marker
- Small amount polyester fiberfill
- Sewing needle and thread
- 2 bamboo skewers
- Clear glitter craft glue
- Small amount birdseed
- Thin wire
- Hot-glue gun

Elves & Skis

1. Cut plastic canvas according to graphs (pages 38–40).

2. Stitch pieces following graphs, reversing two arms before stitching.

3. Add black French Knots for eyes, black Backstitches for mouth and gold Backstitches for buttons over completed background stitching. Where indicated on graph, add a Christmas red Straight Stitch to skis, pulling stitch tight to bring tip up as in photo.

4. Overcast noses and all but the hairline edges of heads with fleshtone. Overcast legs with white and shoes with adjacent colors. Overcast bodies, arms and skis with adjacent colors. With fleshtone, Whipstitch noses to faces where indicated with blue dots on graphs.

5. For hair, cut 16 (6") lengths each of Christmas red and Christmas green yarn. For boy elf, thread red yarn through holes indicated on graph, tying each strand in a knot. Untwist plies of yarn and gently brush yarn, starting at ends and working toward head. Trim ends to desired length.

6. Repeat for girl elf using Christmas green yarn. Using photo as a guide, wrap a 12" length of Christmas red yarn around girl's hair and tie in a bow. Trim ends of bow as desired.

Snowman & Broom

1. Cut plastic canvas according to graphs (pages 39 and 40).

2. Stitch pieces following graphs. One body, one hat and base will remain unstitched. Overcast broom with adjacent colors before adding Christmas green Straight Stitches.

3. Add black French Knots, bittersweet Straight Stitches, and silver Backstitches and Straight Stitches to snowman and Christmas red Straight Stitches to hat over completed background stitching.

4. Whipstitch hat pieces together along sides and top with adjacent colors, making sure to add Christmas red stitches for hatband. Overcast bottom edge of hat front with black.

5. Using white throughout, Whipstitch snowman pieces together along sides and top. Center base between snowman front and back. Whipstitch base

to bottom edges of front and back, Overcasting remaining bottom edges while Whipstitching.

Birds & Letters

1. Cut birds and letters from plastic canvas according to graphs (pages 39 and 40).

2. Stitch pieces following graphs, reversing two birds before stitching. **Note:** *The letter M is the letter W turned upside down.* Add black French Knots for eyes on birds over completed background stitching.

3. Overcast letters with blue/silver cord. Overcast edges of birds with colors indicated on graphs; Overcast remaining edges with adjacent colors.

Finishing

1. Using photo as a guide, wrap about 2⅓ yards ribbon around wreath, beginning and ending at center bottom back. Tie ends in a knot and trim as necessary. Make a multi-looped bow with long tails from remaining ribbon; wrap wire around center of bow and set aside.

2. Using photo as a guide throughout, hot-glue hat at an angle on snowman's head, then glue one bird to top right corner of hat. Glue broom with bristles at the top to snowman's right arm and side. Glue another bird to front of snowman just above bottom edge.

3. Apply glitter glue as desired to broom, hat and snowman. With glue gun, glue snowman to wreath in front of ribbon knot. Attach bow to front bottom of wreath with wire, also threading wire through base of snowman.

4. Center and glue letters to front top of wreath so that bottoms of letters are approximately

¼" apart. Glue bird to ribbon at top of letters.

5. Glue the boy's right arm behind his body and his left arm to body front. Glue head to top edge of body front. Glue upper legs to body back, then glue skis to bottom of feet. Apply glitter glue as desired to skis.

6. For ski poles, cut skewers 6½" long, measuring from pointed end. Glue poles to inside of boy's hands, making sure pointed ends are at the bottom. Glue boy to right side of wreath between letters and bow.

7. Sew short sides of muslin together with a ¼" seam allowance. Sew one end closed, then turn right side out. With black marker, center and print "BIRD SEED" on front of sack. Stuff sack three-fourths full with polyester fiberfill.

8. Glue the girl's left arm behind her body and her right arm to body front. Glue head to top edge of body front. Glue upper legs to body back. Glue birdseed sack under girl's right hand and to body, gluing in gathers at top of sack. Glue girl to left side of wreath between letters and bow.

9. Place a small amount of hot glue in girl's left hand, then cover glue with birdseed. Place glue in top of sack, on dress and on wreath to the right of girl's feet, covering glue with birdseed while glue is still hot. Glue one bird to girl's feet and remaining bird on wreath at right side of birdseed.

— Designed by Trudy Bath Smith

Elf Nose
2 holes x 2 holes
Cut 2

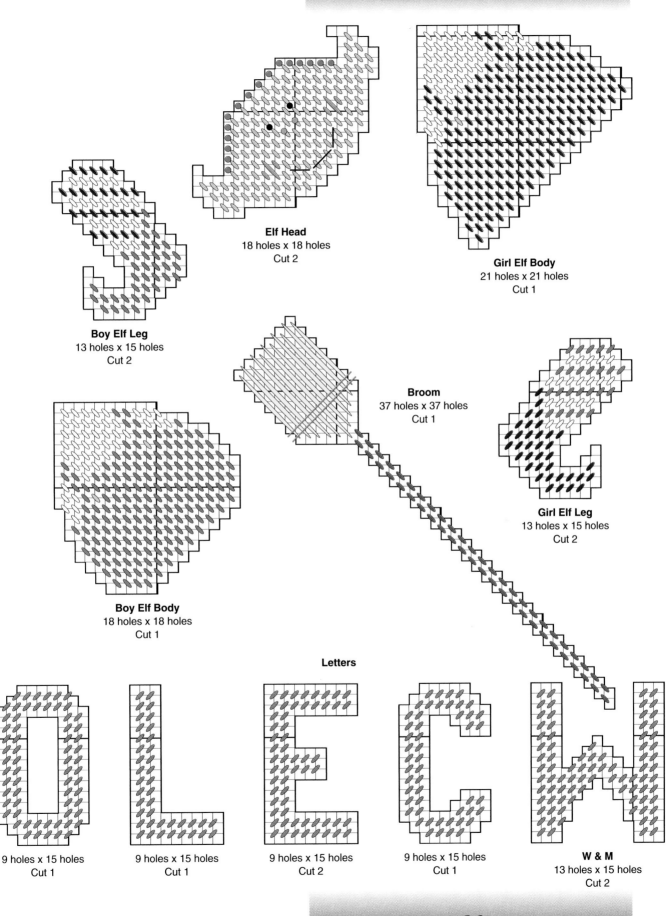

Boy Elf Leg
13 holes x 15 holes
Cut 2

Elf Head
18 holes x 18 holes
Cut 2

Girl Elf Body
21 holes x 21 holes
Cut 1

Broom
37 holes x 37 holes
Cut 1

Girl Elf Leg
13 holes x 15 holes
Cut 2

Boy Elf Body
18 holes x 18 holes
Cut 1

Letters

9 holes x 15 holes
Cut 1

9 holes x 15 holes
Cut 1

9 holes x 15 holes
Cut 2

9 holes x 15 holes
Cut 1

W & M
13 holes x 15 holes
Cut 2

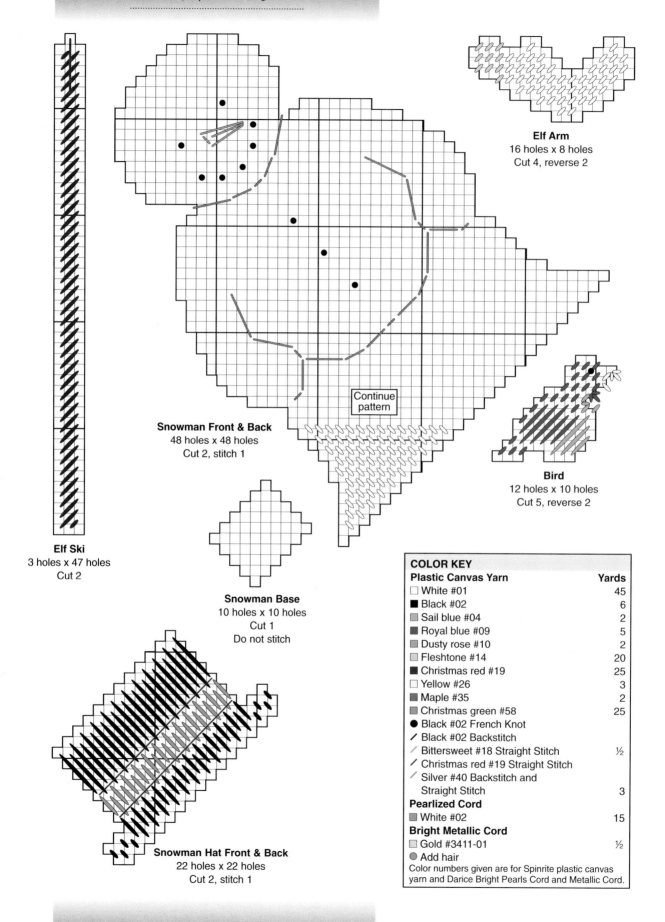

Elf Arm
16 holes x 8 holes
Cut 4, reverse 2

Snowman Front & Back
48 holes x 48 holes
Cut 2, stitch 1

Continue
pattern

Bird
12 holes x 10 holes
Cut 5, reverse 2

Elf Ski
3 holes x 47 holes
Cut 2

Snowman Base
10 holes x 10 holes
Cut 1
Do not stitch

Snowman Hat Front & Back
22 holes x 22 holes
Cut 2, stitch 1

COLOR KEY

Plastic Canvas Yarn	Yards
☐ White #01	45
■ Black #02	6
▨ Sail blue #04	2
▨ Royal blue #09	5
▨ Dusty rose #10	2
▨ Fleshtone #14	20
■ Christmas red #19	25
☐ Yellow #26	3
▨ Maple #35	2
▨ Christmas green #58	25
● Black #02 French Knot	
╱ Black #02 Backstitch	
╱ Bittersweet #18 Straight Stitch	½
╱ Christmas red #19 Straight Stitch	
╱ Silver #40 Backstitch and Straight Stitch	3
Pearlized Cord	
▨ White #02	15
Bright Metallic Cord	
☐ Gold #3411-01	½
● Add hair	

Color numbers given are for Spinrite plastic canvas yarn and Darice Bright Pearls Cord and Metallic Cord.

Snowman
Match Holder

This cheerful snowman holds a stack of long
matches for lighting a toasty warm fire!

Skill Level: Intermediate

Materials

- 3 artist-size sheets 7-count stiff plastic canvas
- Plastic canvas yarn as listed in color key
- 2 (9mm) gold jingle bells
- 2 (18mm) oval movable eyes
- ½" white pompon
- 3 (½") red buttons
- Small amount fiberfill
- Floral clay
- Plastic wrap
- Fireplace matches
- High-temperature glue gun

Cutting & Stitching

1. Cut plastic canvas according to graphs (also see pages 43 and 44).

2. Stitch pieces following graphs, reversing one arm before stitching. Stitch both snow base pieces as one piece. Work all embroidery over completed background stitching.

3. Overcast arms, mitten cuffs, cap cuff and shoes with adjacent colors. Overcast inside and outside edges of snow base with white.

4. Stitch buttons to body front where indicated on graph. Stitch one bell to bottom edge of each cuff (see photo). **Note:** *Straight edge of one cuff will be on the left; straight edge of remaining cuff will be on the right.*

Assembly

1. Using wine throughout, Whipstitch foundation sides together, then sides to foundation bottom. Wrap floral clay in plastic wrap and place in foundation. Whipstitch foundation top to sides. With hole of snow base on the left, glue snow base to top of foundation.

2. With white, Whipstitch wrong sides of body front and back together around side and top edges. Stuff body lightly with fiberfill, then stitch body base to bottom edges of body front and back.

3. Overcast head front and head back between dots with white. With wrong sides together, Whipstitch head front to head back where indicated on graphs with colors given. Whipstitch remaining edges together with adjacent colors.

4. Using black throughout, Overcast bottom edges of lamp; Whipstitch lamp sides together, then top edges of lamp to lamp top. Whipstitch long edges of lamppost pieces together. Overcast lamppost ends. Stuff lamp with fiberfill, then glue one end of lamppost into bottom of lamp.

5. Using photo as a guide through step 7, hold bottom edges of head apart, position over top edge of body and glue in place. Glue mitten cuffs to arms, pompon to tip of hat and movable eyes to face.

6. Glue cap cuff to head front, arms to body sides and feet to bottom of body, making sure bottom edges are even.

7. Glue body to snow base, making sure back edges are even. Glue lamppost to back of foundation, body and head, making sure bottom edges are even.

8. Place matches between arms and body, resting bottom of matches in hole on snow base.

— Designed by Celia Lange Designs

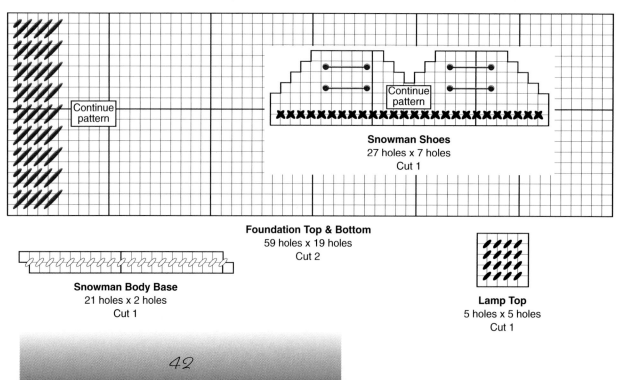

Snowman Shoes
27 holes x 7 holes
Cut 1

Foundation Top & Bottom
59 holes x 19 holes
Cut 2

Snowman Body Base
21 holes x 2 holes
Cut 1

Lamp Top
5 holes x 5 holes
Cut 1

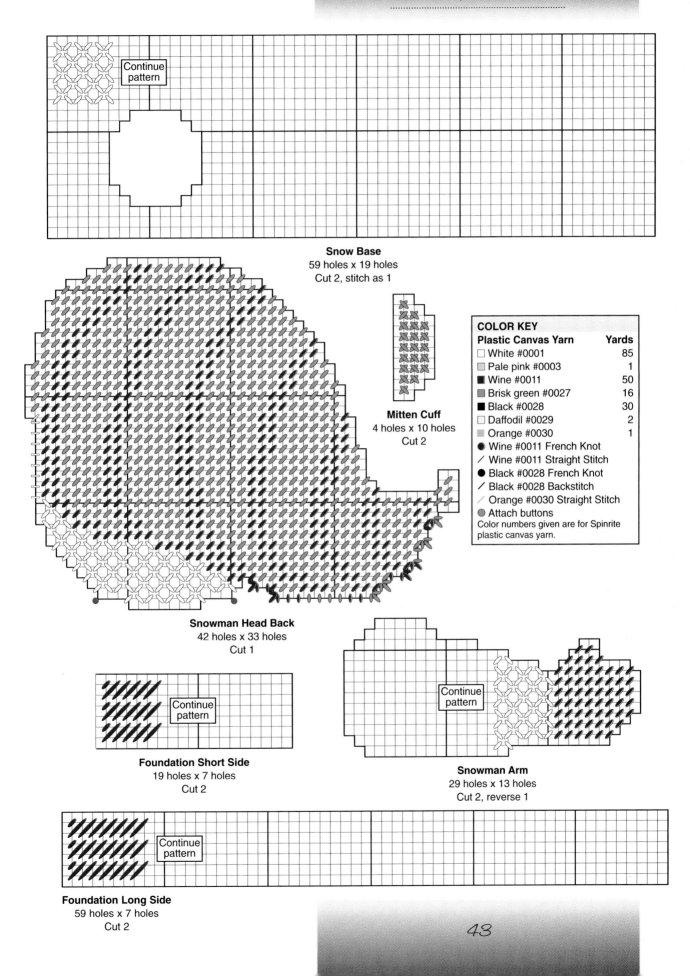

Snow Base
59 holes x 19 holes
Cut 2, stitch as 1

Continue pattern

Mitten Cuff
4 holes x 10 holes
Cut 2

COLOR KEY

Plastic Canvas Yarn	Yards
☐ White #0001	85
☐ Pale pink #0003	1
◨ Wine #0011	50
▨ Brisk green #0027	16
■ Black #0028	30
☐ Daffodil #0029	2
▨ Orange #0030	1
● Wine #0011 French Knot	
╱ Wine #0011 Straight Stitch	
● Black #0028 French Knot	
╱ Black #0028 Backstitch	
╱ Orange #0030 Straight Stitch	
● Attach buttons	

Color numbers given are for Spinrite plastic canvas yarn.

Snowman Head Back
42 holes x 33 holes
Cut 1

Foundation Short Side
19 holes x 7 holes
Cut 2

Continue pattern

Continue pattern

Snowman Arm
29 holes x 13 holes
Cut 2, reverse 1

Foundation Long Side
59 holes x 7 holes
Cut 2

Continue pattern

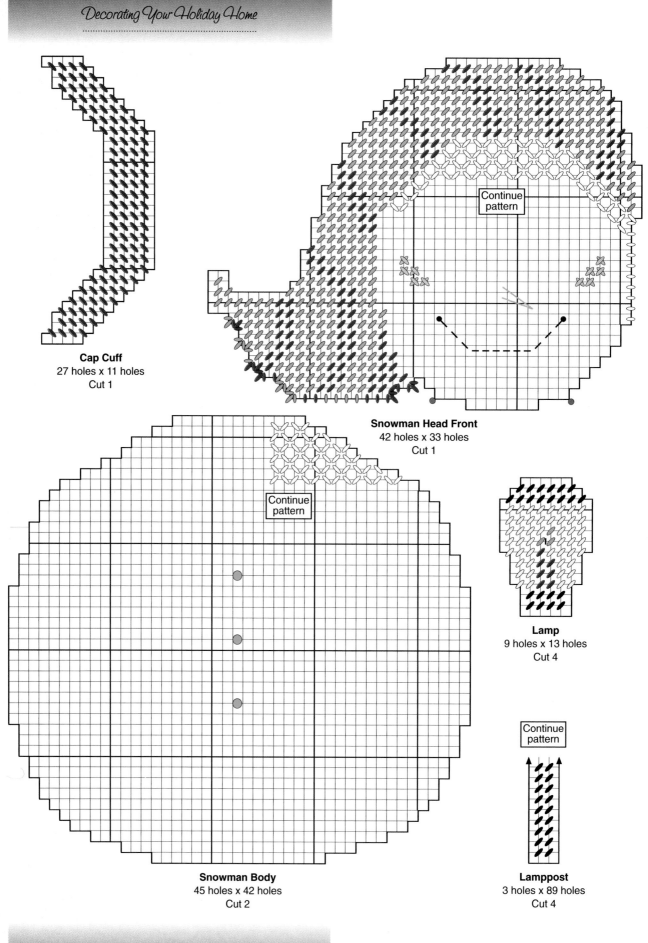

Cap Cuff
27 holes x 11 holes
Cut 1

Snowman Head Front
42 holes x 33 holes
Cut 1

Continue pattern

Continue pattern

Lamp
9 holes x 13 holes
Cut 4

Continue pattern

Snowman Body
45 holes x 42 holes
Cut 2

Lamppost
3 holes x 89 holes
Cut 4

Skill Level: Beginner

Materials

- ½ sheet 10-count plastic canvas
- Ribbon floss as listed in color key
- Metallic ribbon floss as listed in color key
- Acrylic wall hook with plate
- Acrylic rectangular switch plate

Instructions

1. Cut plastic canvas according to graphs (page 55).

2. Continental and Cross Stitch pieces following graphs. Stitch black letters over completed background stitching. Straight Stitch with green, tacking in place where indicated on graphs.

3. Overcast both inside and outside edges with white. Add red metallic ribbon floss, Overcasting in every other hole of plastic canvas as indicated on graphs.

4. Mount stitched pieces in acrylic pieces following manufacturer's instructions.

— Designed by Mary T. Cosgrove

Fleur-de-Lis Mantel Scarf

Decorate your fireplace mantel with this striking mantel scarf. Flecks of gold metallic braid will sparkle in the light of your Christmas tree!

Skill Level: Intermediate

Materials
- 14 sheets 7-count plastic canvas
- Plastic canvas yarn as listed in color key
- 4-ply worsted weight yarn: red with gold thread as listed in color key
- 4mm plastic canvas metallic yarn as listed in color key
- 5 skeins 6-strand embroidery floss: bright Christmas green #700

Project Notes
All graphs, amounts in materials list and yardage amounts given are for sample project. Adjustments may need to be made depending on size of your mantel.

To determine scarf size needed for your mantel, measure width of mantel. To find the number of top panel pieces needed to go across the top of your mantel, divide the width (in inches) by 8 (e.g. 61 ÷ 8 = 7 with 5 left over). Then divide the leftover number by 2 (e.g. 5 ÷ 2 = 2.5). Seven top panels are needed plus two 2½" top end panels—one for each end.

It is not necessary to adjust for a deeper mantel because the scarf does not need to go all the way back. However, the scarf may be adjusted to fit as desired. The depth can be increased by three bars (one Scotch Stitch row) at a time or decreased by three bars at a time until desired size is reached.

Cutting & Stitching
1. Cut plastic canvas according to graphs (page 47–49), cutting the same number of front panels as top panels. Adjust and cut size of top end panels as needed. *Note: Side panels should remain 40 holes long; width should be adjusted following instructions in Project Notes.*

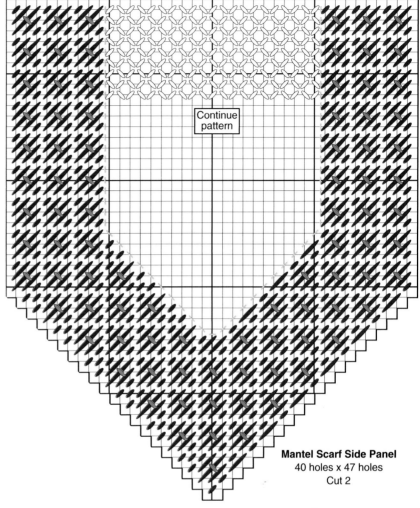

Continue
pattern

Mantel Scarf Side Panel
40 holes x 47 holes
Cut 2

2. Stitch pieces following graphs, working Scotch Stitches and Alternating Continental Stitches first. Work clover stitches over Scotch Stitches, clover fleur-de-lis embroidery and gold Backstitches last.

3. Using gold throughout, Overcast bottom edges of front panels. Overcast side and bottom edges of the two side panels. Overcast top and bottom edges of the two top end panels.

4. Using red tinsel through step 6, Overcast back edges of top panels, then Whipstitch side edges of top panels together.

5. Whipstitch front edges of top panels to top edges of front panels. Whipstitch sides of front panels together.

6. Center and Whipstitch one side edge of a top end panel to one end of assembled top panels. Repeat with remaining top end panel on other end of assembled top panels. Whipstitch top edge of one side panel to each top end panel.

7. Overcast remaining edges with gold.

8. For tassels, tie a small length of gold yarn through loop on each end of bright Christmas

COLOR KEY

Plastic Canvas Yarn		Yards
☐ White #0001		60
▦ Clover #0042		75
╱ Clover #0042 Backstitch		
Christmas Sparkle Yarn		
■ Red tinsel #8300		4 skeins
4mm Plastic Canvas Metallic Yarn		
╱ Gold #PC 1 Backstitch		40

Color numbers given are for Spinrite plastic canvas yarn and Bouquet Christmas Sparkle yarn and Rainbow Gallery Plastic Canvas 7 Metallic Yarn.

green skeins. Wrap gold yarn around skein ½"–¾" from each loop. Cut skeins in half; with gold yarn, attach tassel to points on front and side panels.

— Designed by Celia Lange Designs

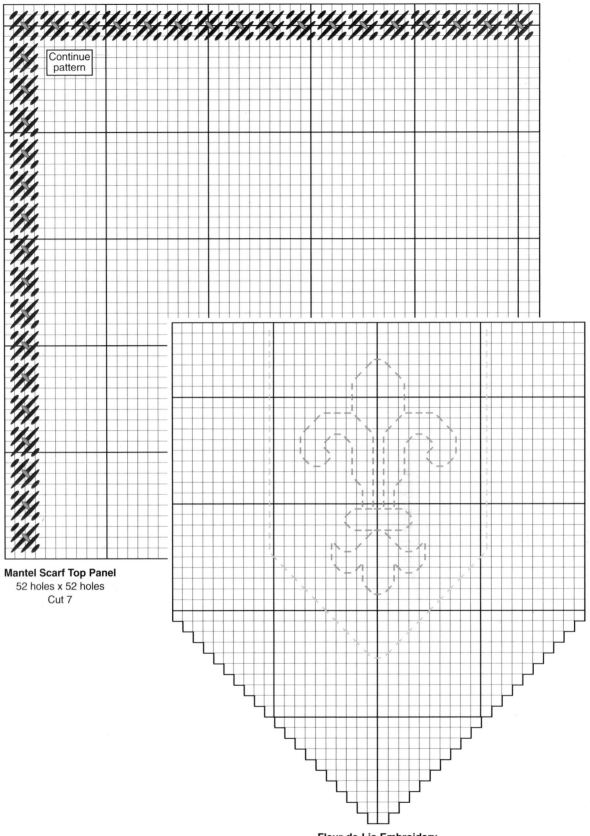

Mantel Scarf Top Panel
52 holes x 52 holes
Cut 7

Continue
pattern

Fleur-de-Lis Embroidery
For front and side panels

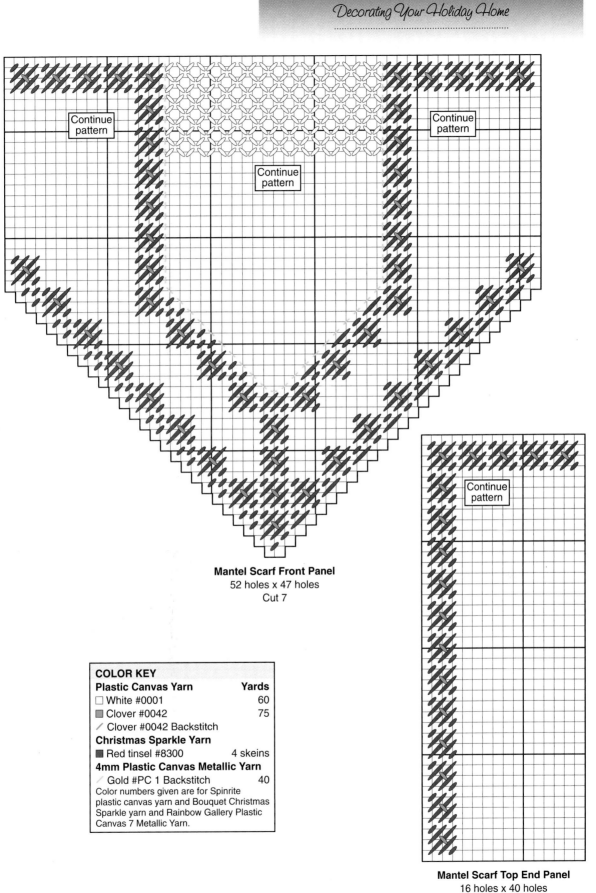

Mantel Scarf Front Panel
52 holes x 47 holes
Cut 7

COLOR KEY

Plastic Canvas Yarn	Yards
☐ White #0001	60
▨ Clover #0042	75
╱ Clover #0042 Backstitch	
Christmas Sparkle Yarn	
■ Red tinsel #8300	4 skeins
4mm Plastic Canvas Metallic Yarn	
╱ Gold #PC 1 Backstitch	40

Color numbers given are for Spinrite
plastic canvas yarn and Bouquet Christmas
Sparkle yarn and Rainbow Gallery Plastic
Canvas 7 Metallic Yarn.

Mantel Scarf Top End Panel
16 holes x 40 holes
Cut 2

Country Button Tree

Make this charming decoration to hang on your craft room door during the holidays!

Skill Level: Beginner

Materials

- 1 sheet 7-count plastic canvas
- Plastic canvas yarn as listed in color key
- Assorted buttons (sample used 37)
- Needle and thread
- 12" ⅛"-wide green satin ribbon

Instructions

1. Cut plastic canvas according to graph.

2. Continental Stitch tree following graph. Overcast edge where indicated with color given. Overcast remaining edges with adjacent colors.

3. With needle and matching thread, sew buttons to tree as desired.

4. Thread ribbon from back to front through holes indicated on graph. Tie ribbon ends in a bow, allowing enough space between bow and plastic canvas for hanging.

— Designed by Michele Wilcox

COLOR KEY

Plastic Canvas Yarn	Yards
■ Red #01	6
☐ Tangerine #11	2
▨ Baby green #26	2
▨ Cerulean #34	2
☐ White #41	3
▨ Plum #59	1
Uncoded area is forest #29 Continental Stitch	30
● Attach ribbon	

Color numbers given are for Uniek Needloft plastic canvas yarn.

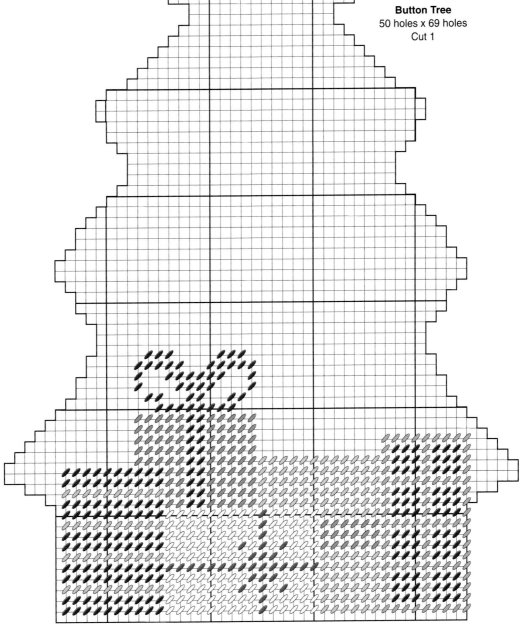

Button Tree
50 holes x 69 holes
Cut 1

Nutcracker Caddy

Here's a solution to keeping control of holiday clutter—a handy magazine caddy!

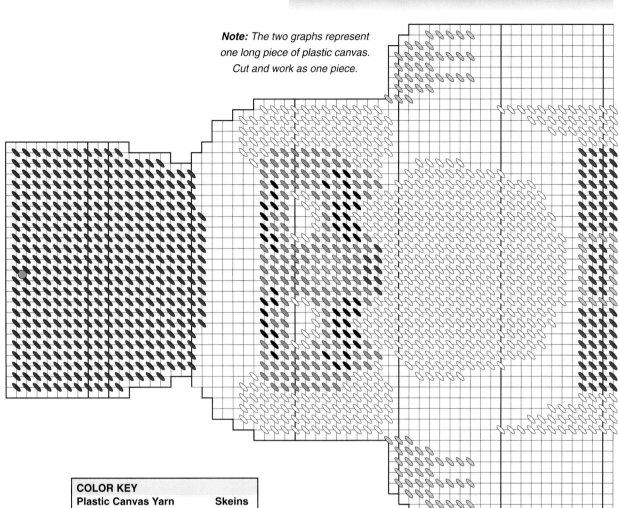

Note: *The two graphs represent one long piece of plastic canvas. Cut and work as one piece.*

COLOR KEY

Plastic Canvas Yarn	Skeins
☐ White #01	7
■ Black #02	1
▨ Baby pink #10	1
☐ Dusty rose #12	1
■ Christmas red #19	1
☐ Gold #27	1
Uncoded areas are royal blue #09 Continental Stitches	1
● Attach tassel	

Color numbers given are for Darice Nylon Plus plastic canvas yarn.

Skill Level: Beginner

Materials
- 3 artist-size sheets 7-count stiff plastic canvas
- Plastic canvas yarn as listed in color key
- 2" gold tassel
- 9" ¼" dowel
- Hot-glue gun

Instructions

1. Cut plastic canvas according to graphs (also see next page). Cut one 58-hole x 32-hole for box bottom which will remain unstitched.

2. Stitch pieces following graphs. On nutcracker, Overcast edges where indicated with colors given. Overcast remaining edges with adjacent colors. With white, Overcast top edges of box sides, Whipstitch sides together, then Whipstitch sides to box bottom.

3. Pull loop of tassel through hole indicated on graph. Glue loop to backside of nutcracker.

4. Center and glue nutcracker to front of box. Glue wooden dowel to center back of nutcracker and to inside of box to support top half of nutcracker.

— Designed by Phyllis Dobbs

Connecting line—do not repeat

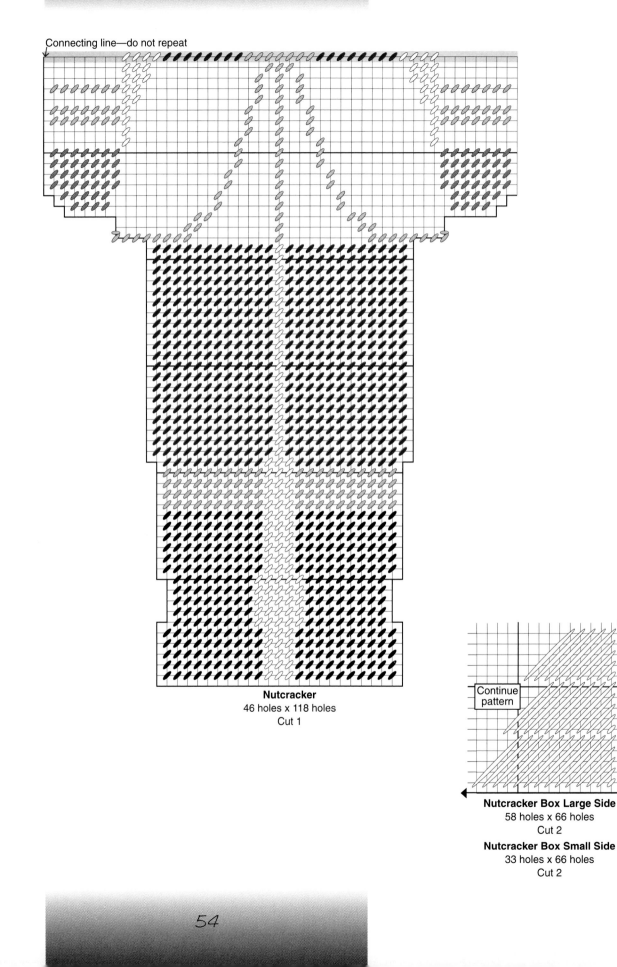

Nutcracker
46 holes x 118 holes
Cut 1

Continue
pattern

Nutcracker Box Large Side
58 holes x 66 holes
Cut 2

Nutcracker Box Small Side
33 holes x 66 holes
Cut 2

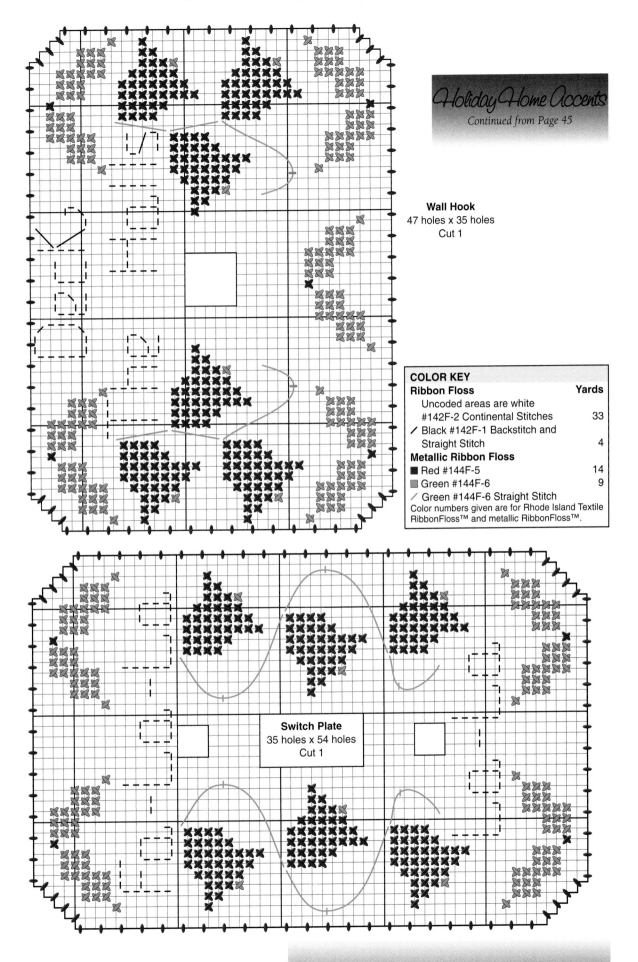

Wall Hook
47 holes x 35 holes
Cut 1

COLOR KEY

Ribbon Floss	Yards
Uncoded areas are white #142F-2 Continental Stitches	33
╱ Black #142F-1 Backstitch and Straight Stitch	4
Metallic Ribbon Floss	
■ Red #144F-5	14
■ Green #144F-6	9
╱ Green #144F-6 Straight Stitch	

Color numbers given are for Rhode Island Textile RibbonFloss™ and metallic RibbonFloss™.

Switch Plate
35 holes x 54 holes
Cut 1

Merry Christmas

*Stitch up a pretty white Christmas scene
to decorate your home during the holidays!
A jolly snowman and brightly lit
Christmas tree add wintry charm.*

COLOR KEY

Plastic Canvas Yarn	Yards
■ Black #00	1
▨ Rose #06	6
▨ Tangerine #11	1
▨ Forest #29	2
☐ White #41	25
■ Crimson #42	7
▨ Camel #43	1
Uncoded area is cerulean #34	
Continental Stitch	25

#3 Pearl Cotton

○ White French Knot	2
╱ Black #310 Backstitch	2
● Black #310 French Knot	
⌒ Nasturtium #349 Lazy Daisy	2
╱ Nasturtium #349 Straight Stitch	
● Nasturtium #349 French Knot	
╱ Russet #434 Straight Stitch	2
Light topaz #726 Straight Stitch	2
○ Light topaz #726 French Knot	
● Light blue #813 French Knot	2
● Light parrot green #907	
○ French Knot	2

Color numbers given are for Uniek Needloft
plastic canvas yarn and DMC #3 pearl cotton.

Skill Level: Beginner

Materials

- ⅔ sheet 7-count plastic canvas
- Plastic canvas yarn as listed in color key
- #3 pearl cotton as listed in color key
- 8" square red frame

Instructions

1. Cut plastic canvas according to graph.

2. Stitch piece following graph, working embroidery over Continental Stitches.

3. Place completed picture in frame.

— Designed by Michele Wilcox

Merry Christmas
53 holes x 53 holes
Cut 1

Let It Snow!

Children especially love this unique
door decoration encouraging
Old Man Winter to let it snow!

LET IT SNOW

Skill Level: Beginner

Materials
- 3 artist-size sheets 7-count stiff plastic canvas
- Worsted weight yarn as listed in color key
- 1 yard red twisted cord
- Heavy cardboard
- Artificial evergreen spray with berries (optional)
- High-temperature glue gun

Instructions

1. Cut plastic canvas according to graphs (see also pages 60 and 61). Cut four 5-hole x 5-hole pieces for support bar end caps. End caps will remain unstitched.

2. Stitch pieces following graphs, reversing two sled runners before stitching. Stitch one side slat following stitch pattern given on right side of graph; stitch remaining side slat following pattern given on left side of graph.

3. Overcast slats and inside and outside edges of crossbar with warm brown. Backstitch slats with country red when Overcasting is completed.

4. With wrong sides together, match edges of two runners and Whipstitch together with country red. Repeat with remaining two runners.

5. With warm brown, Whipstitch long sides of four support bars together, then Whip-stitch one end cap to each end. Repeat with remaining support bar and end cap pieces.

6. Using slats as templates, cut cardboard ¼" smaller on all sides; glue to backside of slats.

7. Glue support bars to insides of runners where indicated on graph. Using photo as a guide, glue slats to support bars and runners.

8. Glue crossbar to slats at top of sled (see photo). Thread ends of cord through holes on crossbar from top to bottom, adjust cord to desired length and knot on wrong side. Trim ends as necessary.

9. *Optional:* Add yarn or ribbon loop at bottom center of crossbar; hang evergreen spray from loop.

—Designed by Celia Lange Designs

Note: *Piece is 102 holes x 19 holes.*

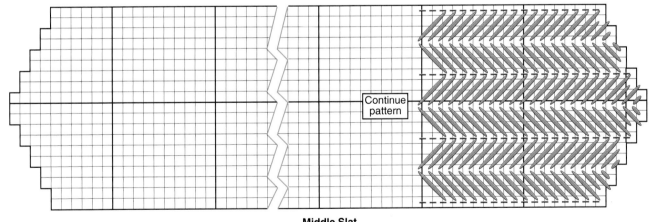

Middle Slat
102 holes x 19 holes
Cut 1

Support Bar
59 holes x 5 holes
Cut 8

COLOR KEY

Worsted Weight Yarn	Yards
▨ Warm brown #336	110
■ Country red #914	90
╱ Country red #914 Backstitch	
⊓ Attach support bar	

Color numbers given are for Coats & Clark Red Heart Classic yarn.

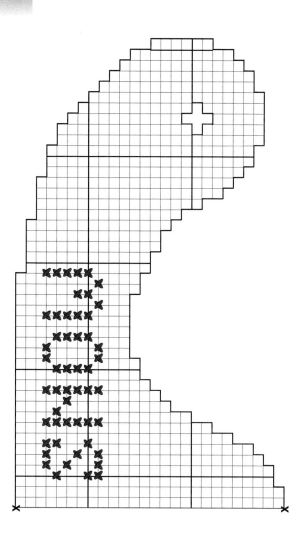

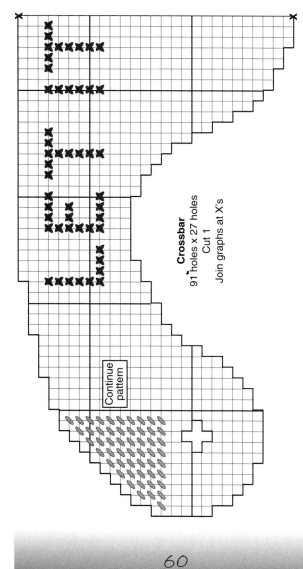

Crossbar
91 holes x 27 holes
Cut 1
Join graphs at X's

Continue pattern

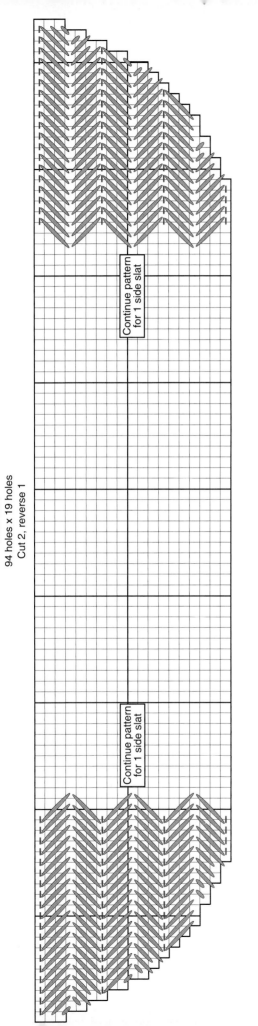

Side Slat
94 holes x 19 holes
Cut 2, reverse 1

Continue pattern
for 1 side slat

Continue pattern
for 1 side slat

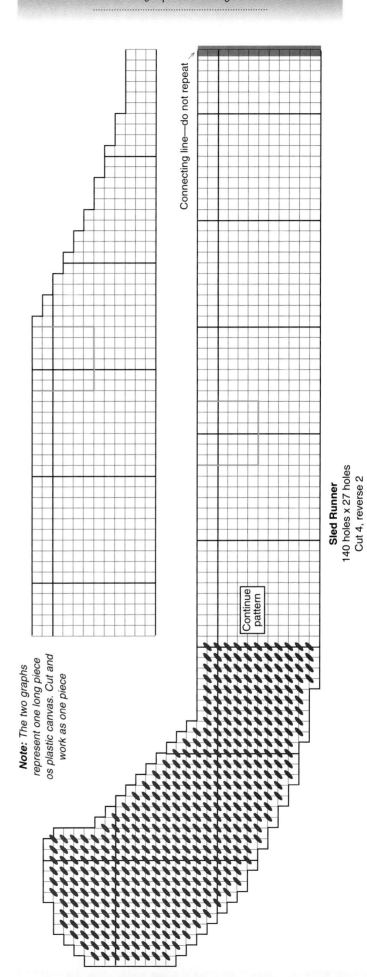

Connecting line—do not repeat

Sled Runner
140 holes x 27 holes
Cut 4, reverse 2

Continue
pattern

Note: *The two graphs represent one long piece os plastic canvas. Cut and work as one piece*

Treasured Gifts

Make your gift-giving extra-special by creating unique and delightful gifts for family and friends. From an attractive German Christmas clock to pretty and practical photo album covers, you'll find wonderfully creative gifts your loved ones will treasure!

German Christmas Clock

Inspired by the treasured cuckoo clocks of Germany, this holiday timepiece will celebrate good friends and good cheer hour after hour!

Skill Level: Intermediate

Materials

- 3 sheets 7-count stiff plastic canvas
- Plastic canvas yarn as listed in color key
- 4mm plastic canvas metallic yarn as listed in color key
- Clock movement
- High-temperature glue gun

Cutting & Stitching

1. Cut plastic canvas according to graphs (at right and pages 66–69). Cut one 62-hole x 24-hole piece for base bottom. Base bottom will remain unstitched.

2. Stitch pieces following graphs, reversing daffodil and brisk green Cross Stitch colors on one side gable. Stitch step top and one step long side only. Bottom seven rows of clock body front, back and sides will remain unstitched.

3. Over completed background stitching, Backstitch numbers with wine; candle flames with orange; and door outline, door window and door handle with black.

4. Alternating wine and white yarn, Overcast top edges of front and side gables from dot to dot. Overcast remaining edges of front and side gables with white yarn.

5. Overcast all trees with white pearl metallic yarn. With almond, Overcast side and bottom edges of clock housing door and inside edges of body front and back.

Assembly

1. Using almond through step 3, Whipstitch clock housing sides to side and bottom edges of clock housing back, then Whipstitch housing sides together at bottom corners.

2. Glue wrong sides of clock body front and clock housing

back together, matching clock stem openings and placing open end of housing at the top.

3. Using Cross Stitches, Whipstitch clock body front and back to clock body sides. Whipstitch clock housing to side and bottom edges of opening on body back, then Whipstitch housing door to top edge of back opening.

4. With curry, Whipstitch roof to top edges of body front, back and sides, then Whipstitch top edges of roof together. Using photo as a guide, glue side gables to top edges of body sides, then glue front gable to top edge of body front.

5. Insert clock body into base top. With white, Whipstitch body to base opening where indicated on graphs.

6. With white, Whipstitch base sides together, then Whipstitch base top to base sides. With white pearl, Whipstitch top to sides in opposite direction of white Whipstitching. Whipstitch base bottom to base sides with white.

7. With white, Whipstitch step sides together then Whipstitch step top to step sides. With white pearl, Whipstitch top to sides in opposite direction of white Whipstitching. Whipstitch step bottom to step sides with white.

8. Install clock movement in housing according to manufacturer's directions.

9. Using photo as a guide, center and glue step to front of base, making sure bottom edges are even and stitched long side is facing front. Glue one small tree to each side of step. Glue large trees to base top and front corners of clock body.

— *Designed by Celia Lange Designs*

COLOR KEY

Plastic Canvas Yarn	Yards
☐ White #0001	45
■ Wine #0011	13
▨ Curry #0014	35
▨ Brisk green #0027	15
■ Black #0028	25
☐ Daffodil #0029	8
☐ Clover #0042	8
▨ Walnut #0047	12
▨ Almond #0056	27
╱ Wine #0011 Backstitch	
╱ Black #0028 Backstitch	
╱ Orange #0030 Backstitch	1
4mm Plastic Canvas Metallic Yarn	
▨ White pearl #PC 10	
⚊ Whipstitch body to base	

Color numbers given are for Spinrite plastic canvas yarn and Rainbow Gallery plastic canvas metallic yarn.

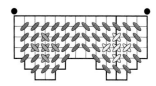

Side Gable
13 holes x 6 holes
Cut 2
Reverse Cross Stitch
colors on 1

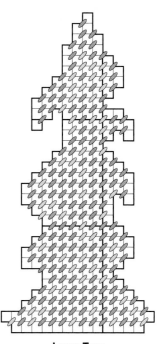

Large Tree
15 holes x 30 holes
Cut 2

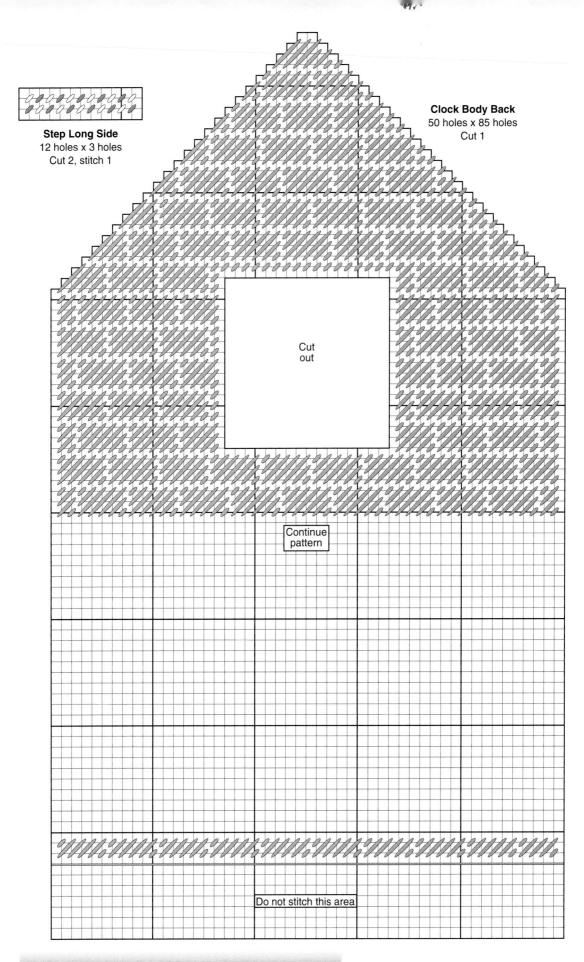

Step Long Side
12 holes x 3 holes
Cut 2, stitch 1

Clock Body Back
50 holes x 85 holes
Cut 1

Cut
out

Continue
pattern

Do not stitch this area

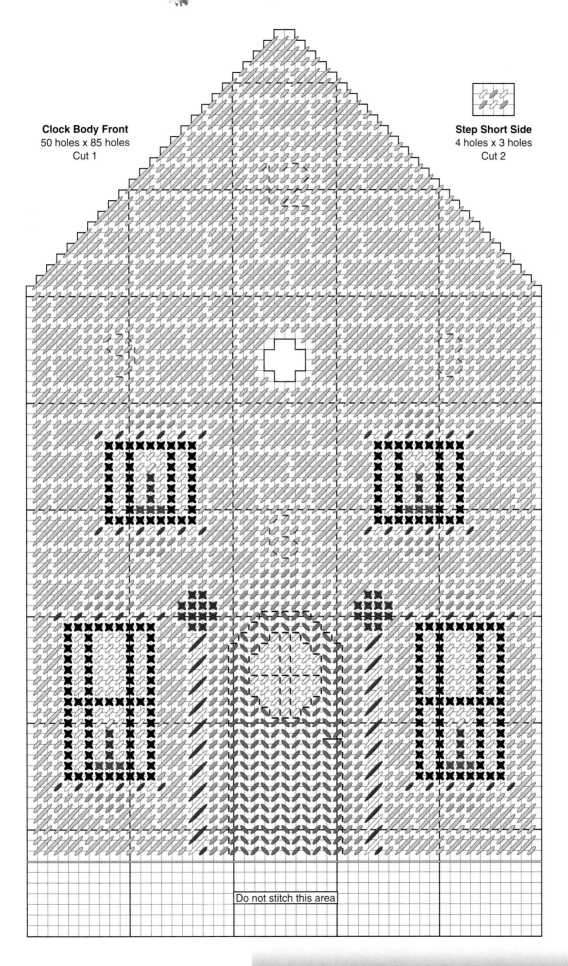

Clock Body Front
50 holes x 85 holes
Cut 1

Step Short Side
4 holes x 3 holes
Cut 2

Do not stitch this area

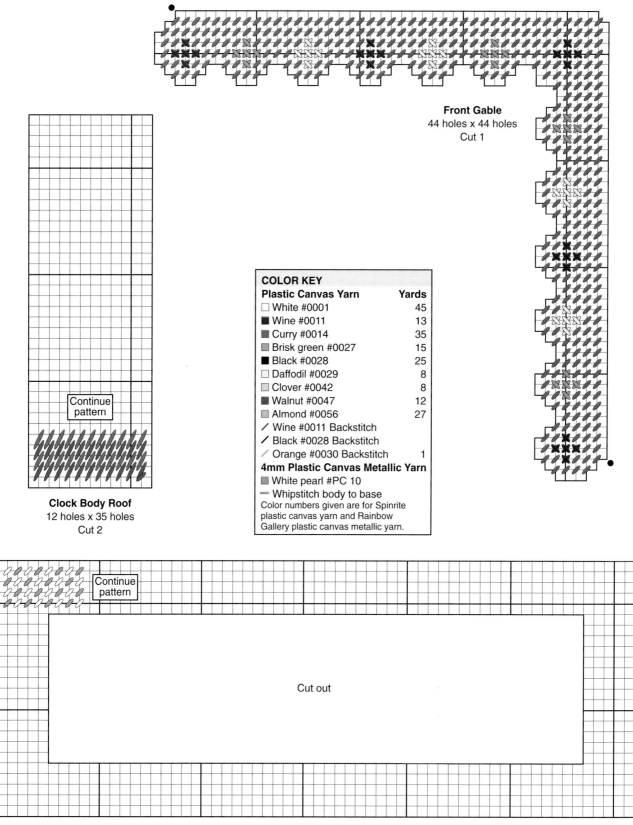

Front Gable
44 holes x 44 holes
Cut 1

Clock Body Roof
12 holes x 35 holes
Cut 2

Continue pattern

COLOR KEY

Plastic Canvas Yarn	Yards
□ White #0001	45
■ Wine #0011	13
▨ Curry #0014	35
■ Brisk green #0027	15
■ Black #0028	25
□ Daffodil #0029	8
□ Clover #0042	8
■ Walnut #0047	12
▨ Almond #0056	27
╱ Wine #0011 Backstitch	
╱ Black #0028 Backstitch	
╱ Orange #0030 Backstitch	1
4mm Plastic Canvas Metallic Yarn	
▨ White pearl #PC 10	
⚊ Whipstitch body to base	

Color numbers given are for Spinrite plastic canvas yarn and Rainbow Gallery plastic canvas metallic yarn.

Continue pattern

Cut out

Base Top
62 holes x 24 holes
Cut 1

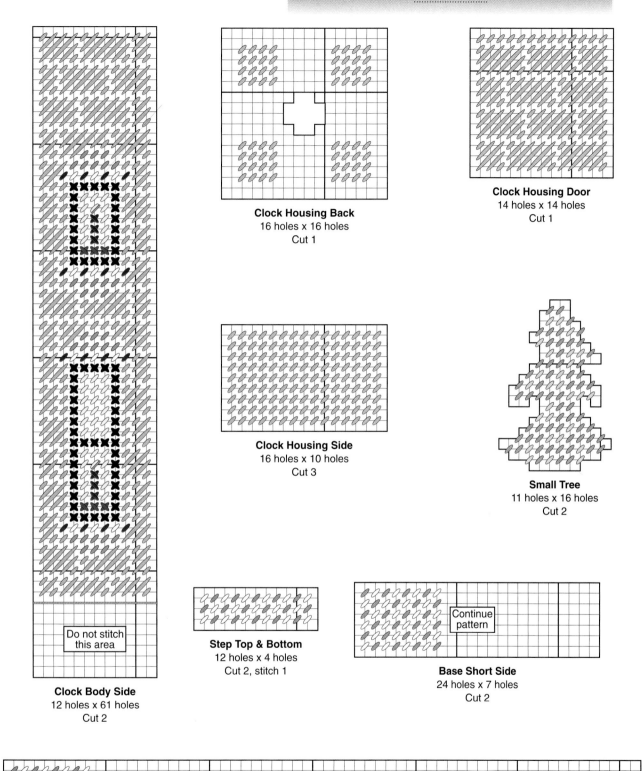

Clock Housing Back
16 holes x 16 holes
Cut 1

Clock Housing Door
14 holes x 14 holes
Cut 1

Clock Housing Side
16 holes x 10 holes
Cut 3

Small Tree
11 holes x 16 holes
Cut 2

Do not stitch
this area

Clock Body Side
12 holes x 61 holes
Cut 2

Step Top & Bottom
12 holes x 4 holes
Cut 2, stitch 1

Continue
pattern

Base Short Side
24 holes x 7 holes
Cut 2

Continue
pattern

Base Long Side
62 holes x 7 holes
Cut 2

Peppermint Candy

Adorned with pink-and-white candy canes, jingle bells and sparkling metallic thread, this pretty tissue box cover is perfect for the holidays!

Skill Level: Beginner

Materials
- 1½ sheets 7-count plastic canvas
- 4-ply 100 percent acrylic craft yarn as listed in color key
- ⅛" metallic ribbon as listed in color key
- 16 (10mm) white jingle bells
- Sewing needle and white thread

Instructions

1. Cut plastic canvas according to graphs.

2. Stitch pieces following graphs. Attach jingle bells with sewing needle and white thread where indicated on graph.

3. Overcast bottom edges of sides with emerald green and inside edges of top with grenadine and pink, alternating colors.

4. Whipstitch sides together with grenadine and pink, alternating colors. Whipstitch top to sides with cherry pink.

— *Designed by Judi Kauffman*

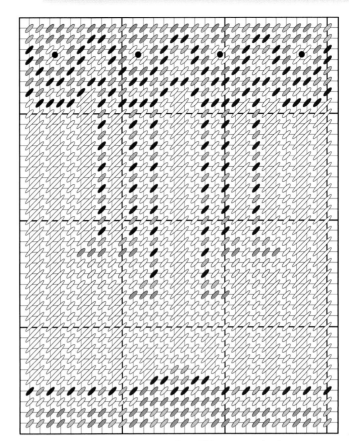

Tissue Box Side
31 holes x 39 holes
Cut 4

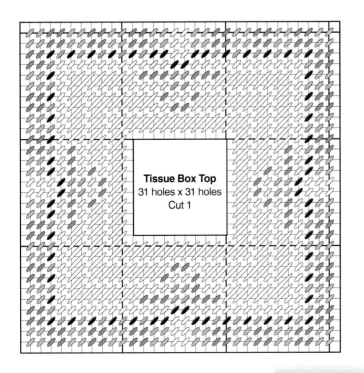

Tissue Box Top
31 holes x 31 holes
Cut 1

COLOR KEY	
Acrylic Craft Yarn	**Yards**
☐ White #1	39
▨ Emerald green #676	20
■ Grenadine #730	30
▨ Pink #737	13
☐ Cherry pink #746	35
⅛" Metallic Ribbon	
☐ Star pink #092	15
● Attach jingle bells	
Color numbers given are for Coats & Clark J. & P. Coats 100 percent acrylic craft yarn and Kreinik ⅛" Ribbon.	

Christmas Memories

Don't let the Christmas spirit slip away once the holiday season is past! Keep your favorite Christmas photographs close at hand in either of these attractive albums!

Green Album

Skill Level: Advanced beginner

Materials

- 2 sheets 7-count plastic canvas
- Plastic canvas yarn as listed in color key
- #5 pearl cotton as listed in color key
- 6" x 7¼" x 2" photo album

Instructions

1. Cut plastic canvas according to graphs (at right and pages 74 and 75). Cut two 13-hole x 49-hole pieces for inner flaps. Inner flaps will remain unstitched.

2. Stitch entire background on front and back covers and spine with brisk green and clover Alternating Continental Stitches following graphs. Stitch embroidery over completed background stitching on spine and front cover only.

3. With brisk green, Whipstitch top edges of front and back covers to long edges of spine.

4. Align back flap with outside edges on wrong side of back cover, then Whipstitch together with brisk green. Continue around outside edges, Overcasting with brisk green and Whipstitching remaining flap into place on front cover while stitching.

— Designed by Celia Lange Designs

ribbon

• 11" x 12" 3-ring-binder–style photo album refill pages

Instructions

1. Cut plastic canvas according to graphs (pages 74, 75 and 83). Cut one 36-hole x 25-hole piece for photo insert back. **Note:** *Width of spine may be increased to accommodate more pages as desired.*

2. Continental Stitch pieces following graphs. Photo insert back will remain unstitched. **Note:** *When stitching front cover, note area to remain unstitched until photo insert back is attached.* Work embroidery over Continental Stitches. For French Knots, wrap ribbon three times around needle.

3. Overcast photo opening on album front with antique gold. Overcast holes on album back and spine front with white.

4. To form a pocket for the photo, with white, Continental Stitch photo insert back to wrong side of album front where indicated on graph.

5. With white, Whipstitch album front to spine front, making sure edge nearest holes on spine front is at the left. Whipstitch spine front to spine side, then spine side to album back, making sure edge nearest holes on back is Whipstitched to spine side. Overcast all remaining edges with white.

6. Insert photo album refill pages inside completed album, aligning holes on refill pages with holes on cover. Thread one end of ribbon through top spine and back-cover holes from front to back; thread other end of ribbon through bottom holes in same manner. Pull ends even at back. Thread both ends through center holes from back to front,

and tie in a bow, catching ribbon length which lies on top.

7. Trim photo as needed and insert into pocket on front cover.

— Designed by Darla Fanton

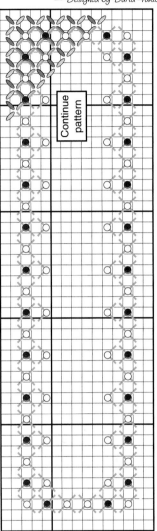

Green Album Cover Spine
49 holes x 15 holes
Cut 1

COLOR KEY	
WHITE ALBUM	
Plastic Canvas Yarn	**Yards**
☐ White #0001	165
■ Brisk green #0027	8
Ribbon Floss	
● Red #142F-12 French Knot	5
╱ Evergreen #142F-19 Backstitch	8
╱ Wine #142F-24 Backstitch	6
╱ Leave unstitched until attaching photo insert back	
Color numbers given are for Spinrite plastic canvas yarn and Rhode Island Textile RibbonFloss.	

White Album

Skill Level: Advanced beginner

Materials

• 2 sheets stiff 7-count plastic canvas

• Plastic canvas yarn as listed in color key

• Ribbon floss as listed in color key

• 5 yards metallic ribbon floss: antique gold #144F-12

• 1⅛ yards ¼"-wide red satin

Cut out

White Album Front Cover
68 holes x 81 holes
Cut 1

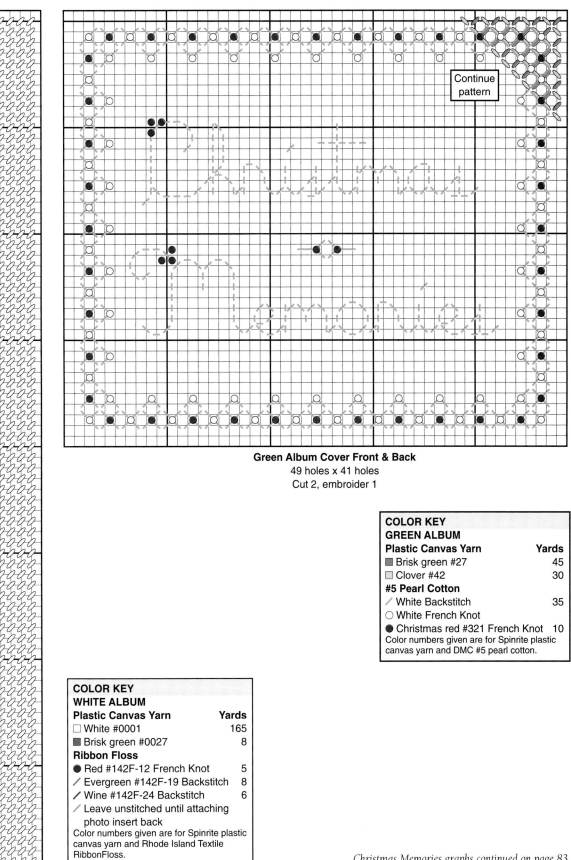

Green Album Cover Front & Back
49 holes x 41 holes
Cut 2, embroider 1

Continue pattern

COLOR KEY
GREEN ALBUM

Plastic Canvas Yarn	Yards
■ Brisk green #27	45
□ Clover #42	30

#5 Pearl Cotton

	Yards
╱ White Backstitch	35
○ White French Knot	
● Christmas red #321 French Knot	10

Color numbers given are for Spinrite plastic canvas yarn and DMC #5 pearl cotton.

COLOR KEY
WHITE ALBUM

Plastic Canvas Yarn	Yards
□ White #0001	165
■ Brisk green #0027	8

Ribbon Floss

	Yards
● Red #142F-12 French Knot	5
╱ Evergreen #142F-19 Backstitch	8
╱ Wine #142F-24 Backstitch	6
╱ Leave unstitched until attaching photo insert back	

Color numbers given are for Spinrite plastic canvas yarn and Rhode Island Textile RibbonFloss.

White Album Spine Side
5 holes x 81 holes
Cut 1

Christmas Memories graphs continued on page 83

Ribbons & Bows Frame

Give grandparents this special frame holding photographs of their grandchildren. They're sure to proudly display it all throughout the season!

FRAME BRACE
Cut 2 from
white cardboard

Glue this side
of fold line.

- - - - - - - - Fold Line - - - - - - - -

Do not glue this area.

COLOR KEY

Acrylic Craft Yarn	Yards
☐ Natural #111	12
☐ Emerald #676	19
☐ Paddy green #686	18
■ Bright red #901	12
‖ Attach bow ends	

Color numbers given are for J. & P. Coats 100 percent acrylic craft yarn.

Skill Level: Beginner

Materials
- ½ sheet 7-count plastic canvas
- 4-ply 100 percent acrylic craft yarn as listed in color key
- Heavyweight white cardboard
- Craft glue

Instructions

1. Cut plastic canvas according to graphs.

2. Stitch pieces following graphs. Overcast bow with bright red. On frame, Overcast bottom edge of striped ribbon area with white and all other edges with emerald.

3. Fold bow ends back and tack with bright red yarn to backside of bow where indicated on graph. With bright red, attach bow to center top of frame at top edge of striped ribbon area (see photo).

4. Cut cardboard slightly smaller than stitched frame piece. Lay cardboard under completed frame and position photos. Glue or tape photos in place.

5. Apply a thin layer of glue to areas around photos and glue to back of picture frame. Let dry.

6. For frame brace, cut two pieces of cardboard using pattern given. Matching edges, glue pieces together where indicated on pattern. Fold remaining sections of cardboard back to form wings. Center and glue wing section to back of frame. Allow to dry thoroughly.

— Designed by Judi Kauffman

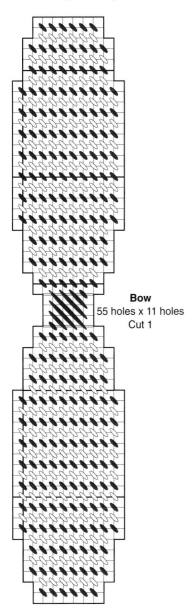

Bow
55 holes x 11 holes
Cut 1

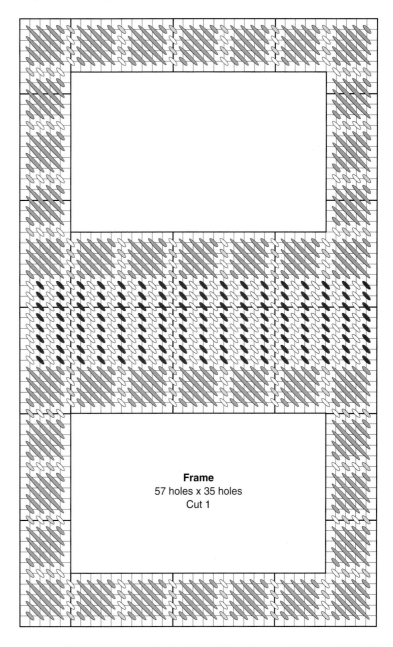

Frame
57 holes x 35 holes
Cut 1

Swiss Cottages

These charming cottages make lovely decorations all throughout the winter season. Each can also double as a box for holding a gift or sweets!

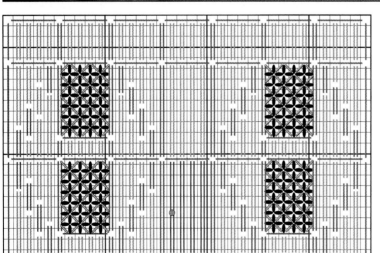

Small Cottage Long Side
36 holes x 23 holes
Cut 2

Large Cottage Chimney Side
7 holes x 10 holes
Cut 4

COLOR KEY

Plastic Canvas Yarn		Yards
■ Red #01		10
▨ Maple #13		80
■ Brown #15		130
□ White #41		70
╱ Black #00 Backstitch		30
● Maple #13 French Knot		
#5 Pearl Cotton		
╱ Snow white Backstitch		26

Color numbers given are for Uniek Needloft plastic canvas yarn and DMC #5 pearl cotton.

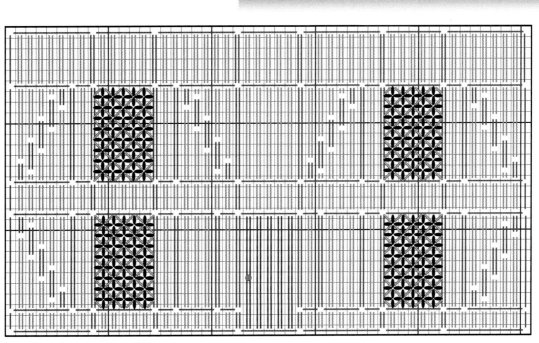

Large Cottage Long Side
51 holes x 29 holes
Cut 2

Skill Level: Advanced beginner

Materials
- 3 artist-size sheets 7-count stiff plastic canvas
- Plastic canvas yarn as listed in color key
- #5 pearl cotton as listed in color key
- #16 tapestry needle
- Hot-glue gun

Instructions

1. Cut plastic canvas according to graphs (also see pages 80 and 81). Cut one 51-hole x 25-hole piece for large cottage bottom and one 36-hole x 21-hole piece for small cottage bottom. Cottage bottoms will remain unstitched.

2. Stitch pieces following graphs in the following stitches and colors: red Long Stitch, maple Long Stitch, black Backstitch, snow white pearl cotton Backstitch, brown Long Stitch, white yarn Long Stitch. Add maple French Knot to door last.

3. Using brown throughout, Overcast top edges of small cottage long sides and then top edges from blue dot to blue dot on small cottage short sides. Whipstitch sides together, then sides to small box bottom.

4. With white, Whipstitch top edges of small roof together, then Overcast remaining roof edges.

5. With white, Overcast top edges of small chimney sides, then Whipstitch sides together. Glue chimney into hole of roof.

6. Repeat steps 3–5 for large cottage.

— *Designed by Angie Arickx*

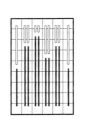

Small Cottage Chimney Side
6 holes x 9 holes
Cut 4

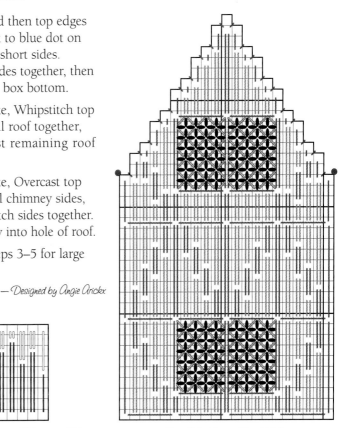

Small Cottage Short Side
21 holes x 38 holes
Cut 2

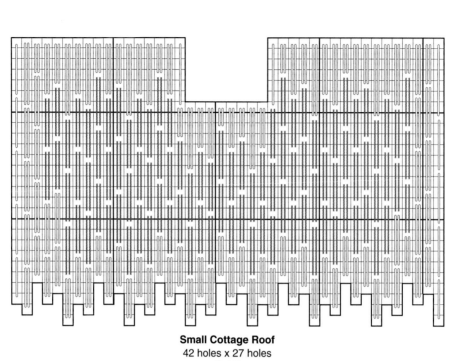

Small Cottage Roof
42 holes x 27 holes
Cut 2

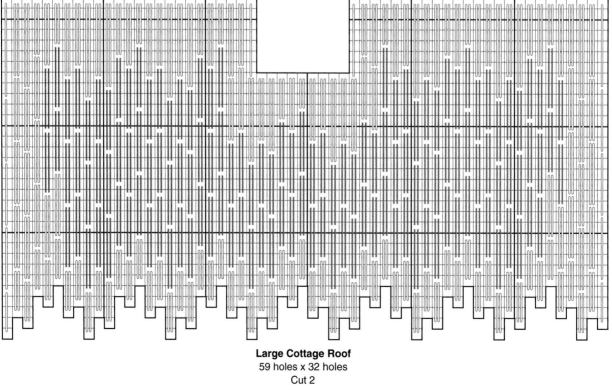

Large Cottage Roof
59 holes x 32 holes
Cut 2

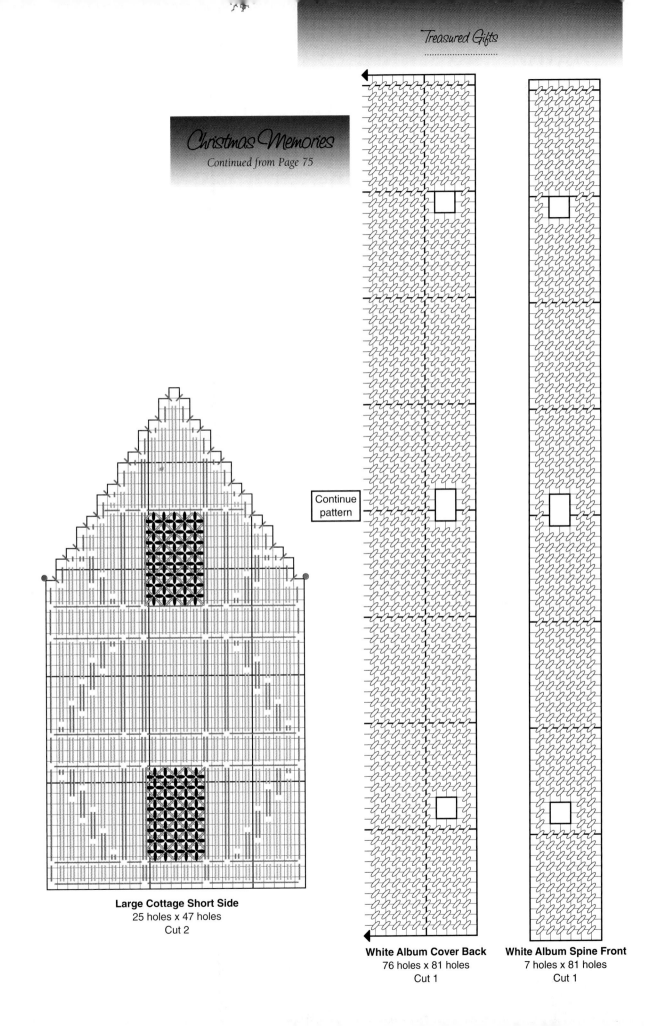

Christmas Memories
Continued from Page 75

Continue
pattern

Large Cottage Short Side
25 holes x 47 holes
Cut 2

White Album Cover Back
76 holes x 81 holes
Cut 1

White Album Spine Front
7 holes x 81 holes
Cut 1

The Christmas Kitchen

Holiday entertaining is one of the year's most rewarding endeavors. A warm and inviting kitchen, filled with tempting smells and decorated with cheerful holiday decorations, will add to your seasonal celebrating!

Christmas Canister Covers

*Place your everyday canisters inside this set
of colorful holiday canister covers to bring
Christmas cheer into your kitchen!*

Skill Level: Intermediate

Sizes

Tea Canister: 4½" wide x 6" tall with bow

Coffee Canister: 5½" wide x 7¼" tall with bow

Sugar Canister: 6¾" wide x 8¾" tall with bow

Flour Canister: 8" wide x 10½" tall with bow

Materials

- 10 artist-size sheets 7-count stiff plastic canvas
- 1 sheet 7-count soft plastic canvas
- Worsted weight yarn as listed in color key
- 4mm plastic canvas metallic yarn as listed in color key
- White unlined index cards
- High-temperature glue gun

Cutting & Stitching

1. Cut ribbon tails, bow loops, bow centers and tags from soft plastic canvas; cut tags, canister sides, lid sides and lid tops from stiff plastic canvas according to graphs (pages 85–91).

2. From stiff plastic canvas, cut one 27-hole x 27-hole piece for tea canister bottom, one 34-hole x 34-hole piece for coffee canister bottom, one 42-hole x 42-hole piece for sugar canister bottom and one 50-hole x 50-hole piece for flour canister bottom.

3. Continental Stitch flour and tea canister bottoms with cherry red; Continental Stitch sugar and coffee canister bottoms with emerald.

4. Stitch remaining pieces following graphs, working Slanting Gobelin Stitches for ribbons on canister sides, lid sides and lid tops first, then stitch main design areas. Stitch gold metallic yarn Straight Stitch over completed background stitching.

5. Overcast edges of smaller cutout areas on tags with adjacent colors as indicated on graphs. Overcast remaining outer and inner edges with gold.

6. Overcast ribbon tails, bow centers and loops with adjacent colors.

Assembly

1. For flour and tea canisters, Overcast top edges of canister sides and bottom edges of lid sides with cherry red, except ribbon areas which should be Overcast with ribbon color.

2. Using cherry red, Whipstitch flour and tea canister sides together together; Whipstitch canister sides to corresponding bottoms with cherry red and matching ribbon-area colors.

3. Using cherry red, Whipstitch flour lid sides together and tea lid sides together, then Whipstitch lid tops to corresponding lid sides, using ribbon color in ribbon areas.

4. Repeat steps 1–3 for sugar and coffee canisters, replacing cherry red with emerald.

5. Glue short edges of one bow loops piece together at center back, wrap corresponding bow center around center of bow loops and glue, making sure all seams are in back. Repeat with remaining bows.

6. Glue tails to center of corresponding lid tops, then glue bows to tails. ***Note:*** *Design on lid top will match with design on only one lid side. Position bow so this side is used as front of canister lid.*

7. For labels, using tags as templates, cut index cards slightly smaller than tags. Center and print "Flour," "Sugar," "Coffee" and "Tea" (or label as desired) on corresponding labels so words will show in openings. Glue labels to back of tags. Glue tag to top of canister, making sure gold yarn is centered under small opening on tag.

— Designed by Celia Lange Designs

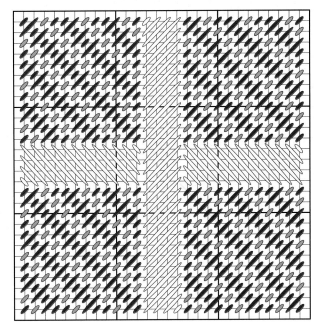

Tea Lid Top
29 holes x 29 holes
Cut 1 from stiff

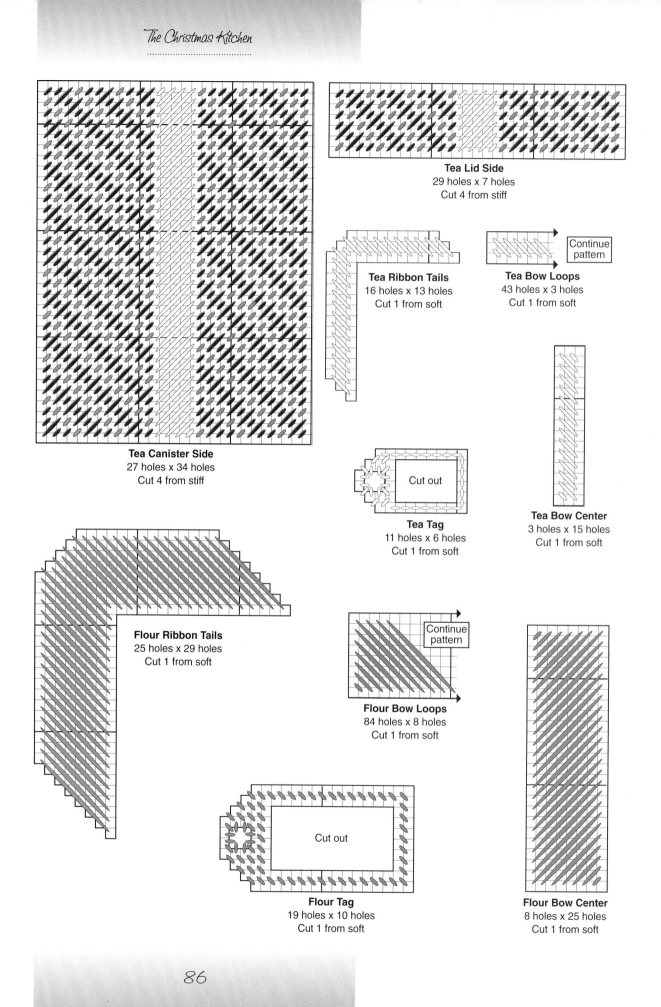

Tea Lid Side
29 holes x 7 holes
Cut 4 from stiff

Tea Ribbon Tails
16 holes x 13 holes
Cut 1 from soft

Tea Bow Loops
43 holes x 3 holes
Cut 1 from soft

Continue pattern

Tea Canister Side
27 holes x 34 holes
Cut 4 from stiff

Cut out

Tea Tag
11 holes x 6 holes
Cut 1 from soft

Tea Bow Center
3 holes x 15 holes
Cut 1 from soft

Flour Ribbon Tails
25 holes x 29 holes
Cut 1 from soft

Continue pattern

Flour Bow Loops
84 holes x 8 holes
Cut 1 from soft

Cut out

Flour Tag
19 holes x 10 holes
Cut 1 from soft

Flour Bow Center
8 holes x 25 holes
Cut 1 from soft

Flour Lid Top
52 holes x 52 holes
Cut 1 from stiff

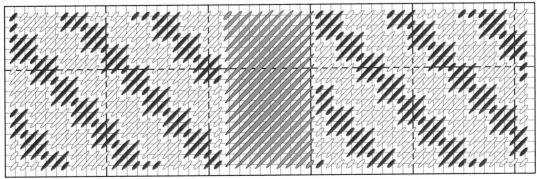

Flour Lid Side
52 holes x 16 holes
Cut 4 from stiff

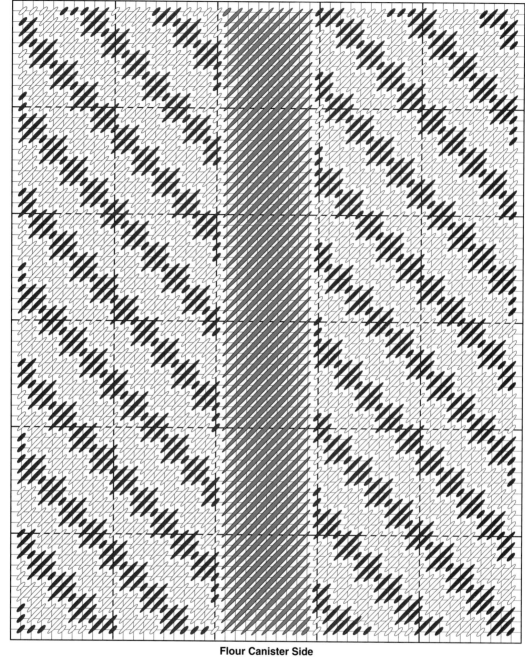

Flour Canister Side
50 holes x 60 holes
Cut 4 from stiff

Coffee Bow Center
4 holes x 15 holes
Cut 1 from soft

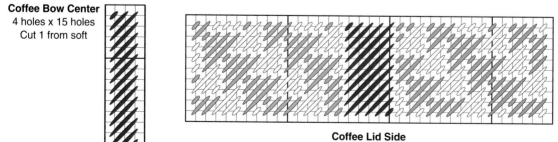

Coffee Lid Side
36 holes x 10 holes
Cut 4 from stiff

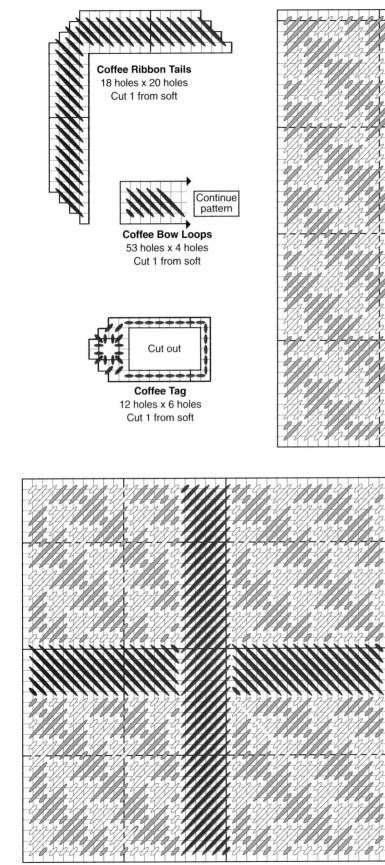

Coffee Ribbon Tails
18 holes x 20 holes
Cut 1 from soft

Continue pattern

Coffee Bow Loops
53 holes x 4 holes
Cut 1 from soft

Cut out

Coffee Tag
12 holes x 6 holes
Cut 1 from soft

Coffee Canister Side
34 holes x 41 holes
Cut 4 from stiff

Coffee Lid Top
36 holes x 36 holes
Cut 1 from stiff

COLOR KEY	
Worsted Weight Yarn	**Yards**
☐ White #01	250
▨ Emerald #676	310
▪ Cherry red #310	290
4mm Plastic Canvas Metallic Yarn	
Gold #PC1 Straight Stitch	8

Color numbers given are for Coats & Clark
Red Heart Classic yarn and Rainbow Gallery
Plastic Canvas 7 Metallic Yarn.

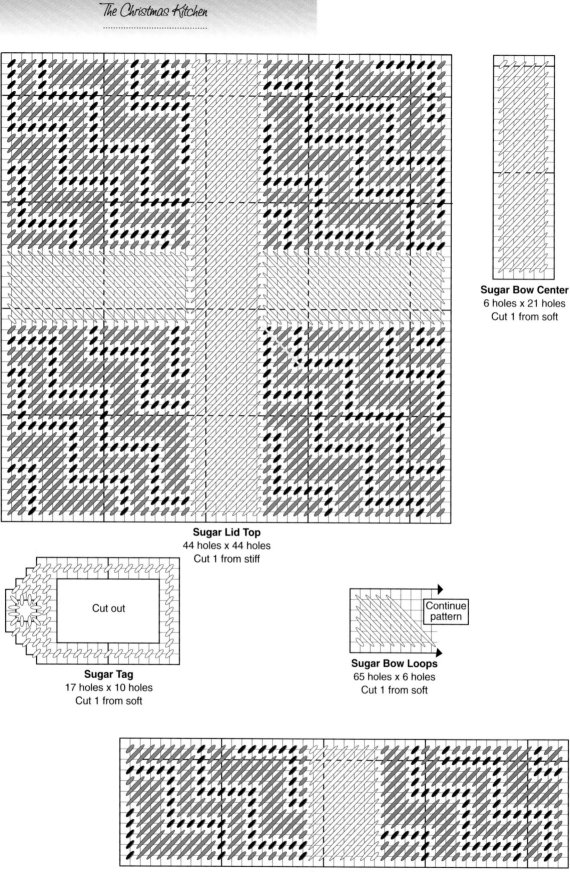

Sugar Bow Center
6 holes x 21 holes
Cut 1 from soft

Sugar Lid Top
44 holes x 44 holes
Cut 1 from stiff

Cut out

Sugar Tag
17 holes x 10 holes
Cut 1 from soft

Continue
pattern

Sugar Bow Loops
65 holes x 6 holes
Cut 1 from soft

Sugar Lid Side
44 holes x 12 holes
Cut 4 from stiff

Sugar Ribbon Tails
21 holes x 19 holes
Cut 1 from soft

COLOR KEY	
Worsted Weight Yarn	**Yards**
☐ White #01	250
■ Emerald #676	310
■ Cherry red #310	290
4mm Plastic Canvas Metallic Yarn	
Gold #PC1 Straight Stitch	8

Color numbers given are for Coats & Clark Red Heart Classic yarn and Rainbow Gallery Plastic Canvas 7 Metallic Yarn.

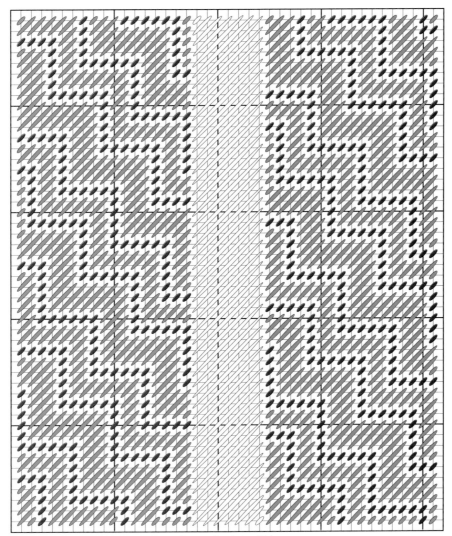

Sugar Canister Side
42 holes x 49 holes
Cut 4 from stiff

Mr. & Mrs. Santa Bear

These sweet Santa bears add a charming touch to an ordinary basket. They're quick and easy to stitch too!

Skill Level
Beginner

Materials
- ⅓ sheet 7-count plastic canvas
- Plastic canvas yarn as listed in color key
- Plastic canvas metallic cord as listed in color key
- #16 tapestry needle
- Medium-size basket
- Hot-glue gun

Instructions

1. Cut plastic canvas according to graphs (at right).

2. Stitch pieces following graphs, working French Knots over completed background stitching.

3. Overcast heart wreath with holly and arms with adjacent colors. Overcast edges of bears where indicated with colors given. Overcast remaining edges with adjacent colors.

4. Thread a 12" length of gold metallic cord from back to front through holes indicated on graph and tie in a bow. Tie ends in a knot, trimming as necessary.

5. Using photo as a guide, glue arms to bears and hands to wreath. Glue bears and wreath to basket.

— Designed by Angie Arickx

COLOR KEY

Plastic Canvas Yarn	Yards
■ Black #00	2
■ Christmas red #02	6
■ Gold #17	4
□ Holly #27	3
□ Beige #40	1
□ White #41	4
● Black #00 French Knot	
● Christmas red #02 French Knot	
Plastic Canvas Metallic Cord	
□ Gold #01	½
○ Thread gold cord	

Color numbers given are for Uniek
Needloft plastic canvas yarn and
plastic canvas metallic cord.

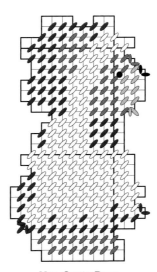

Mrs. Santa Bear
13 holes x 23 holes
Cut 1

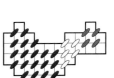

Mr. Santa Bear Arm
11 holes x 5 holes
Cut 1

Mrs. Santa Bear Arm
10 holes x 6 holes
Cut 1

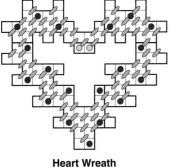

Heart Wreath
16 holes x 14 holes
Cut 1

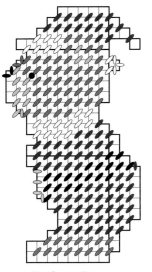

Mr. Santa Bear
13 holes x 24 holes
Cut 1

Christmas Star Cookies

Ingredients

- 2 cups confectioners' sugar
- 5 egg whites
- ⅛ teaspoon salt
- 2 teaspoons cinnamon
- 1 teaspoon grated lemon rind
- 1 lb ground unblanched almonds

Instructions

Preheat oven to 300 degrees. Sift confectioners' sugar; set aside.
Whip egg whites and salt until stiff but not dry. Gradually add
sugar, continuing to whip. Whipping constantly, add cinnamon
and lemon rind. Set aside one-third of mixture. Into remaining
two-thirds, fold almonds.

Dust a board lightly with confectioners' sugar. Pat dough to ⅓"
thickness; do not roll—it is too delicate. If batter sticks to
fingers, dust fingers lightly with confectioners' sugar. Cut cakes
with star shape cutter. Glaze tops with reserved mixture. Bake
on greased cookie sheet 20 minutes. Yields 45 1½" stars.

Santa Claus Coasters

Serve up drinks for kids and adults alike on these friendly Santa Claus coasters! He'll be the hit of your holiday party!

Skill Level: Intermediate

Materials

- 1 sheet 10-count plastic canvas
- 6-strand embroidery floss as listed in color key
- Tapestry needle

Instructions

1. Cut plastic canvas according to graphs. Cut one 36-hole x 13-hole piece for coaster box bottom.

2. Stitch pieces following graphs, using 12 strands floss. Box bottom will remain unstitched.

3. For coasters, Overcast cap area with Christmas red and remaining edges with very light pearl gray.

4. For box, Overcast top edge of box front with adjacent colors and top edges of sides and back with Christmas red. Whipstitch front and back to sides, then Whipstitch bottom to front, back and sides with Christmas red.

—*Designed by Phyllis Dobbs*

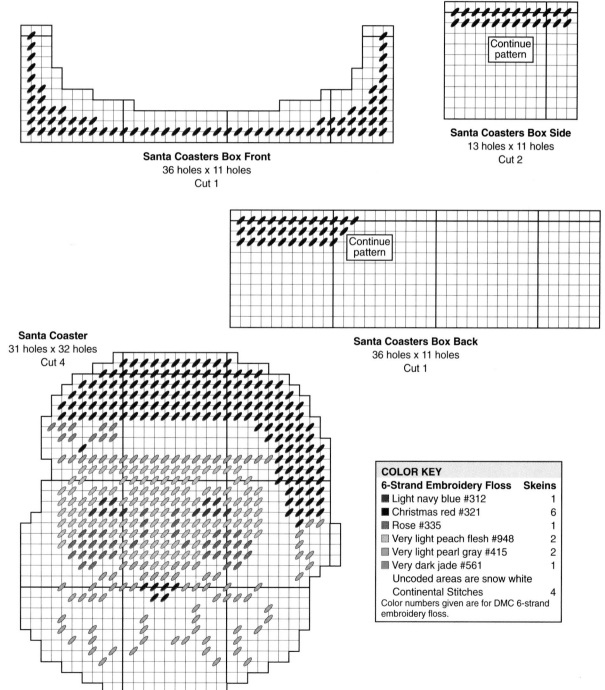

Santa Coasters Box Front
36 holes x 11 holes
Cut 1

Santa Coasters Box Side
13 holes x 11 holes
Cut 2

Santa Coaster
31 holes x 32 holes
Cut 4

Santa Coasters Box Back
36 holes x 11 holes
Cut 1

COLOR KEY	
6-Strand Embroidery Floss	**Skeins**
■ Light navy blue #312	1
■ Christmas red #321	6
▨ Rose #335	1
▨ Very light peach flesh #948	2
▨ Very light pearl gray #415	2
▨ Very dark jade #561	1
Uncoded areas are snow white	
Continental Stitches	4
Color numbers given are for DMC 6-strand embroidery floss.	

Holly & Chickadee

This beautiful table set will serve you well for many years during the winter months. Stitch as many or as few place settings as needed.

Skill Level: Advanced beginner

Materials
- 1 sheet 7-count plastic canvas
- ½ sheet 10-count plastic canvas
- ½ sheet 14-count plastic canvas
- 4-ply yarn as listed in color key
- 6-strand embroidery floss as listed in color key

Instructions

1. For coasters, cut four pieces from 7-count plastic canvas according to graphs. Two pieces will remain unstitched.

2. Continental Stitch coasters following graphs. Over completed Continental Stitching, use black yarn to Straight Stitch legs. Use 6 strands embroidery floss for Backstitching.

3. Whipstitch unstitched pieces to backside of stitched pieces with adjacent colors, working two stitches per hole. Use additional stitches as needed to conceal canvas completely.

4. For candle cozy, cut one 102-hole x 30-hole piece from

10-count plastic canvas. Using 12 strands embroidery floss for Continental Stitching, center either design on canvas and stitch following graph.

5. Stitch remaining background area with horizon blue and white, extending snow line to ends of piece, overlapping last three rows on each end to form cozy. Over completed background stitching, use 12 strands floss to Straight Stitch legs and 6 strands floss for Backstitching.

6. For napkin rings, cut one 96-hole x 30-hole piece from

14-count plastic canvas per napkin ring. Using 6 strands embroidery floss for Continental Stitch and Straight Stitch (for legs)

and 3 strands for Backstitching, stitch and finish as for candle cozy in steps 4 and 5.

— Designed by Karen Wiant

COLOR KEY	
COASTERS	
4-ply Yarn	**Yards**
■ Black	4
□ Off-white	4
▨ Charcoal heather	3
□ Silver heather	3
▨ Steel	3
■ Coffee	3
▨ Nutmeg	3
□ Light beige	3
▨ Forest green	5
▨ Cameo rose	2
■ Red	4
▨ Horizon blue	10
□ White	10
╱ Black Backstitch (legs and feet)	
6-Strand Embroidery Floss	
╱ Black #310 Backstitch	
╱ Ultra dark green pistachio green #890 Backstitch	
CANDLE COZY & NAPKIN RINGS	
6-Strand Embroidery Floss	**Skeins**
■ Black #310	2
□ Ecru	2
▨ Pewter gray #317	1
□ Light steel gray #318	1
▨ Very light pearl gray #415	1
■ Very dark coffee brown #898	1
▨ Medium beige brown #840	1
□ Ultra very light beige brown #842	1
▨ Ultra dark pistachio green #890	1
▨ Medium antique mauve #316	1
■ Very dark Christmas red #498	1
▨ Medium antique blue #931	3
□ White	3
╱ Black #310 Backstitch (legs and feet)	
╱ Black #310 Backstitch	
╱ Ultra dark pistachio green #890 Backstitch	

Color numbers given are for DMC 6-strand embroidery floss.

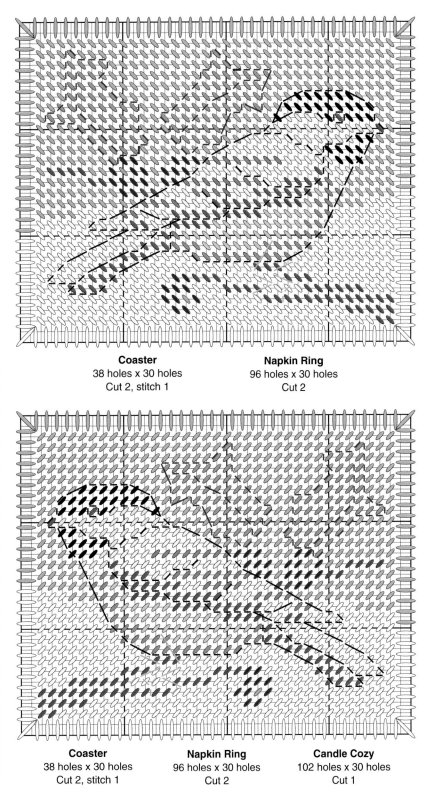

Coaster
38 holes x 30 holes
Cut 2, stitch 1

Napkin Ring
96 holes x 30 holes
Cut 2

Coaster
38 holes x 30 holes
Cut 2, stitch 1

Napkin Ring
96 holes x 30 holes
Cut 2

Candle Cozy
102 holes x 30 holes
Cut 1

Striped Star Candy Dish

Fill this festive star-shaped candy dish with melt-in-your-mouth candies as a treat for holiday guests!

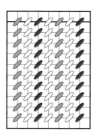

Short Side
8 holes x 11 holes
Cut 2

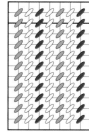

Large Side
8 holes x 12 holes
Cut 4

Skill Level: Beginner

Materials
- 2 (5") plastic canvas stars
- ¼ sheet 7-count plastic canvas
- Plastic canvas yarn as listed in color key
- 4mm metallic braid as listed in color key
- #18 tapestry needle
- 12" ¼"-wide red satin ribbon

Project Note
When working with metallic braid, keep braid smooth and flat. To prevent twisting and tan-gling, guide braid between thumb and forefinger of free hand. Drop needle occasionally to let braid unwind.

Instructions
1. Cut top loop from stars, leaving smaller loop intact. Cut side pieces from plastic canvas according to graphs.

2. Stitch pieces following graphs, Overcasting top edges of stars from dot to dot with white. Overcast at stars' top points under loops; do not Overcast loops.

3. Using white through step 4, Whipstitch short edges of four large and two small sides together with small sides at each end, forming a strip.

4. Whipstitch side strip to stars around side and bottom edges from dot to dot. Overcast top edges of sides.

5. Thread ribbon through loops at top of stars and tie into a bow, trimming tails as desired.

— Designed by Kathy Wirth

Star
Stitch 2

Country Angel

This sweet angel will add a folk-art look to your kitchen. Use her to hold napkins, cutlery or other items on a buffet table.

Skill Level: Advanced beginner

Materials

- 2 sheets almond 7-count plastic canvas
- 2 sheets maroon 7-count plastic canvas
- Plastic canvas yarn as listed in color key
- 6-strand embroidery floss as listed in color key
- #16 tapestry needle
- ⅔ yard plastic canvas metallic cord: gold #01
- 10 (13mm) star pony beads #1167: gold sparkle #310
- 8 (8mm) faceted craft beads #710: crystal #006
- Gold chenille stem
- 4 heart-shaped brass charms #1052

Instructions

1. Cut two basket sides each from almond and maroon plastic canvas and one almond basket bottom according to graphs (at right and page 105). Cut one 6-hole x 90-hole basket handle from almond.

2. Stitch almond basket sides only following graph, working embroidery over completed background stitching. Almond basket bottom and handle and maroon basket sides will remain unstitched.

3. Place one maroon basket side behind each stitched almond basket side, matching edges. Using eggshell through step 4,

Whipstitch basket sides together.

4. Overcast long edges of handle. Center and Whipstitch short handle edges to top edge of basket sides at side seams; continue Whipstitching remaining top edges of maroon and almond basket sides together while attaching handle. Whipstitch basket bottom to sides.

5. Sew two brass charms to each side of handle where handle and basket meet.

6. Cut two 12" lengths of gold cord. Thread one length from front to back through one of the holes indicated on graph; knot end on backside.

7. Thread five gold star pony beads alternated with four crystal faceted beads on cold cord, so that a gold star is on each end. Thread remaining end through remaining hole indicated on graph. Using photo as a guide, adjust cord to desired length; knot end on backside, trimming excess cord. Repeat with remaining cord and beads on opposite side of basket.

8. For halo, cut two 4" lengths of gold chenille stem. Thread ends of one length through holes indicated on graph. Using photo as a guide, adjust halo to desired length; overlap and twist chenille ends on inside of basket. Repeat with remaining chenille stem on opposite side of basket.

— *Designed by Adele Mogavero*

Country Angel graphs continued on page 106

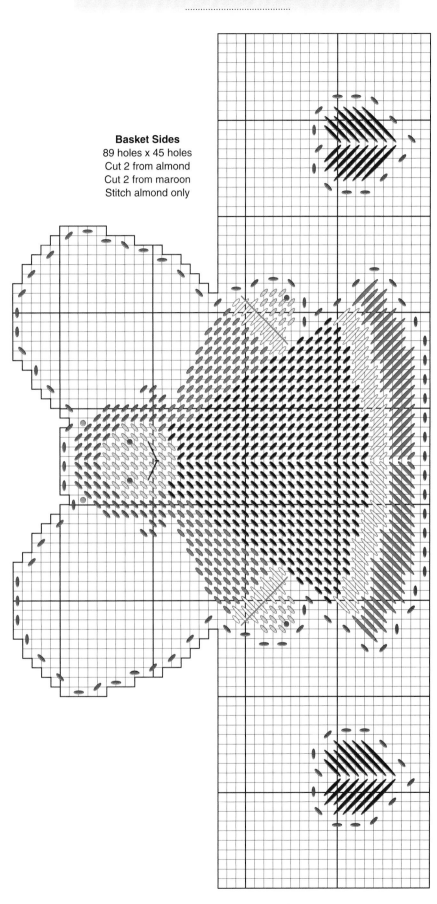

Basket Sides
89 holes x 45 holes
Cut 2 from almond
Cut 2 from maroon
Stitch almond only

COLOR KEY

Plastic Canvas Yarn	Yards
■ Burgundy #03	40
■ Cinnamon #14	10
□ Straw #19	10
■ Forest #29	30
▨ Fleshtone #56	5
Eggshell #39 Overcasting	15
╱ Forest #29 Straight Stitch	
6-Strand Embroidery Floss	
╱ Red Backstitch and Straight Stitch	1
● Brown French Knot	1
● Attach gold cord	
● Attach halo	

Color numbers given are for Uniek Needloft plastic canvas yarn.

Whether you're serving up warm apple cider or refreshing eggnog, these pretty coasters will give your entertaining an extra-special touch!

Skill Level: Intermediate

Materials
- 4 sheets 7-count plastic canvas
- Worsted weight yarn as listed in color key
- ¼ sheet white craft foam
- High-temperature glue gun

Instructions

1. Cut plastic canvas according to graphs (at right and page 104).

2. Stitch pieces following graphs. Do not add Backstitches to lid sides and corners at this time. Add clusters of honey gold and yellow French Knots as desired to center of one coaster only. Overcast all coasters with cardinal.

3. Using lid top as a template, cut craft foam to fit lid shape.

4. Using country red through step 6, Whipstitch box sides together in the following order: large side, corner, small side, corner. Repeat stitching order until all box sides and corners are Whipstitched together. Whipstitch bottom to sides and corners.

5. Whipstitch lid sides and corners together following the same order as for box sides and corners. Whipstitch lid top to lid sides and corners. Work honey gold and paddy green Backstitches on lid sides and corners, Backstitching around connecting edges as well (see photo).

6. Overcast bottom edges of lid sides and corners and top edges of box sides and corners.

7. Glue craft foam to wrong side of lid top. Center and glue poinsettia with French Knots to right side of lid top. Place remaining four poinsettia coasters in box.

— Designed by Celia Lange Designs

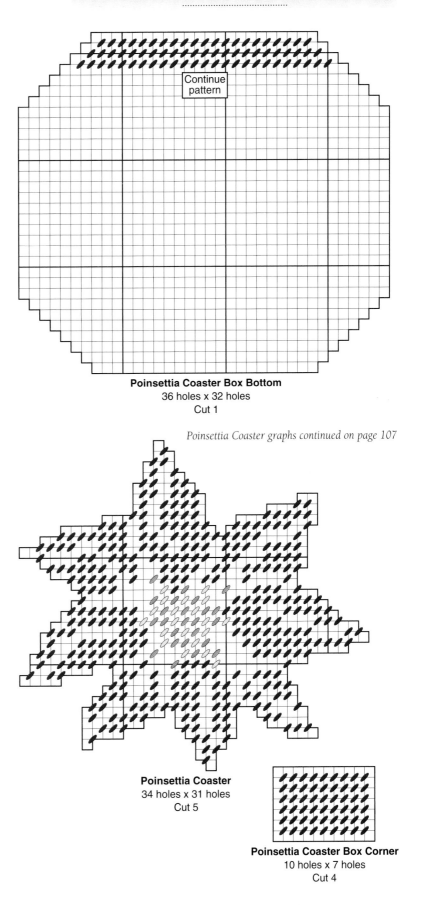

Poinsettia Coaster Box Bottom
36 holes x 32 holes
Cut 1

Poinsettia Coaster graphs continued on page 107

Poinsettia Coaster
34 holes x 31 holes
Cut 5

Poinsettia Coaster Box Corner
10 holes x 7 holes
Cut 4

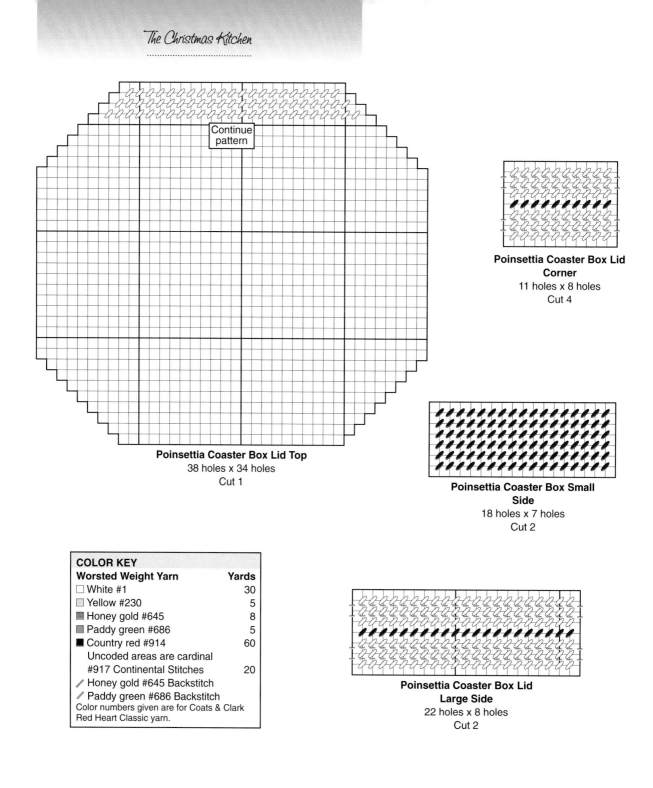

Poinsettia Coaster Box Lid Top
38 holes x 34 holes
Cut 1

Poinsettia Coaster Box Lid Corner
11 holes x 8 holes
Cut 4

Poinsettia Coaster Box Small Side
18 holes x 7 holes
Cut 2

COLOR KEY

Worsted Weight Yarn	Yards
☐ White #1	30
☐ Yellow #230	5
▨ Honey gold #645	8
▨ Paddy green #686	5
■ Country red #914	60
Uncoded areas are cardinal #917 Continental Stitches	20
⁄ Honey gold #645 Backstitch	
⁄ Paddy green #686 Backstitch	

Color numbers given are for Coats & Clark Red Heart Classic yarn.

Poinsettia Coaster Box Lid Large Side
22 holes x 8 holes
Cut 2

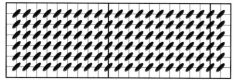

Poinsettia Coaster Box Large Side
22 holes x 7 holes
Cut 2

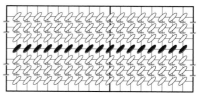

Poinsettia Coaster Box Lid Small Side
18 holes x 8 holes
Cut 2

Country Angel

Continued from page 101

Basket Bottom
52 holes x 41 holes
Cut 1 from almond
Do not stitch

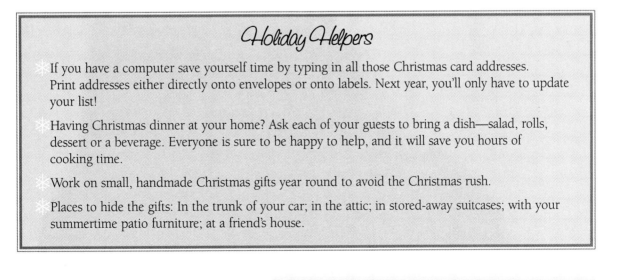

Holiday Helpers

❄ If you have a computer save yourself time by typing in all those Christmas card addresses. Print addresses either directly onto envelopes or onto labels. Next year, you'll only have to update your list!

❄ Having Christmas dinner at your home? Ask each of your guests to bring a dish—salad, rolls, dessert or a beverage. Everyone is sure to be happy to help, and it will save you hours of cooking time.

❄ Work on small, handmade Christmas gifts year round to avoid the Christmas rush.

❄ Places to hide the gifts: In the trunk of your car; in the attic; in stored-away suitcases; with your summertime patio furniture; at a friend's house.

Stockings & Stocking Stuffers

From festive and colorful stockings to hang on the mantel to more than a dozen easy-to-make stocking stuffers, this collection of Christmas stockings and gifts will bring you hours of stitching and gift-giving delight!

Folk-Art Stripe Stocking

You'll want to include this handsome stocking in your Christmas decorating!

Skill Level: Beginner

Materials

- 2 sheets 7-count plastic canvas
- Plastic canvas yarn as listed in color key
- 9" jute

Instructions

1. Cut plastic canvas according to graph.

2. Stitch stockings following graph, reversing one before stitching. Add extra paddy green horizontal and vertical Straight Stitches as needed to cover canvas.

3. Add cardinal Lazy Daisy Stitches and Straight Stitches for bows on wreaths over completed background stitching.

4. Using honey gold throughout, overcast top edges of stockings. With wrong sides together and matching edges, Whipstitch front to back along side and bottom edges.

5. Thread jute through stocking seam where indicated on graph; tie ends in a knot.

— Designed by Nancy Marshall

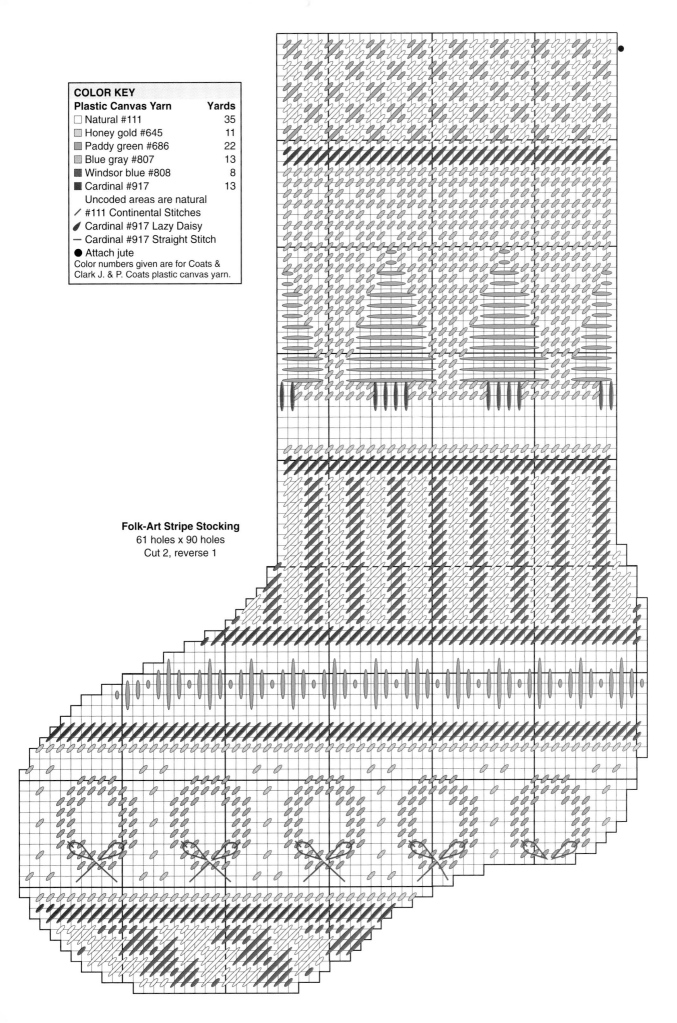

COLOR KEY

Plastic Canvas Yarn	Yards
☐ Natural #111	35
☐ Honey gold #645	11
☐ Paddy green #686	22
☐ Blue gray #807	13
■ Windsor blue #808	8
■ Cardinal #917	13

Uncoded areas are natural

╱ #111 Continental Stitches

❮ Cardinal #917 Lazy Daisy

— Cardinal #917 Straight Stitch

● Attach jute

Color numbers given are for Coats & Clark J. & P. Coats plastic canvas yarn.

Folk-Art Stripe Stocking
61 holes x 90 holes
Cut 2, reverse 1

Ice Crystals

This sparkling stocking will add an elegant touch to your mantel this holiday season.

Skill Level: Intermediate

Materials
- ½ sheet 14-count soft plastic canvas
- 6-strand embroidery floss as listed in color key
- Medium (#16) braid as listed in color key
- 5 yards ¹⁄₁₆" metallic ribbon: light aqua #4639
- Tapestry needle
- 2 (11" x 14") pieces deep turquoise velvet
- 2 (11" x 14") pieces pale turquoise cotton
- Turquoise sewing thread

Project Note

When working with metallic ribbon or braid, keep ribbon and braid smooth and flat. To prevent twisting and tangling, guide ribbon and braid between thumb and forefinger of free hand. Drop needle occasionally to let ribbon and braid unwind.

Instructions

1. Cut plastic canvas according to graphs (right and page 113).

2. Stitch pieces following graphs. Overcast pieces with light aqua ¹⁄₁₆" metallic ribbon, stitching three times in outer corners for complete coverage.

3. With ¹⁄₁₆" metallic ribbon, sew corner of dangle indicated on graph to cuff where indicated on graph.

4. Using pattern given, cut two stockings from velvet, reversing one, and two stockings from cotton, reversing one, joining A to A and B to B before cutting.

5. With right sides together, stitch around sides and bottom of velvet stockings with a ½" seam allowance, leaving top edges open. Repeat with cotton stockings for lining. Trim seam allowances and clip curves. Turn

velvet stocking right side out.

6. For hanger, cut a 12" length of deep turquoise floss and a 12" length of light aqua braid. Twist both lengths together, fold in half and set aside.

7. Turn top edges of both stocking and liner under ½". With turquoise sewing thread, tack

top edge of stitched cuff ⅛" from top front edge of velvet stocking.

8. Sew loop to inside top back edge of stocking. Insert lining with wrong side out into stocking. Hand-stitch lining to stocking along top edges.

— Designed by Judi Kauffman

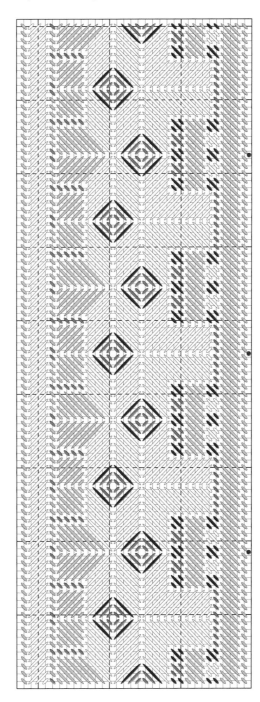

Ice Crystals Cuff
91 holes x 33 holes
Cut 1

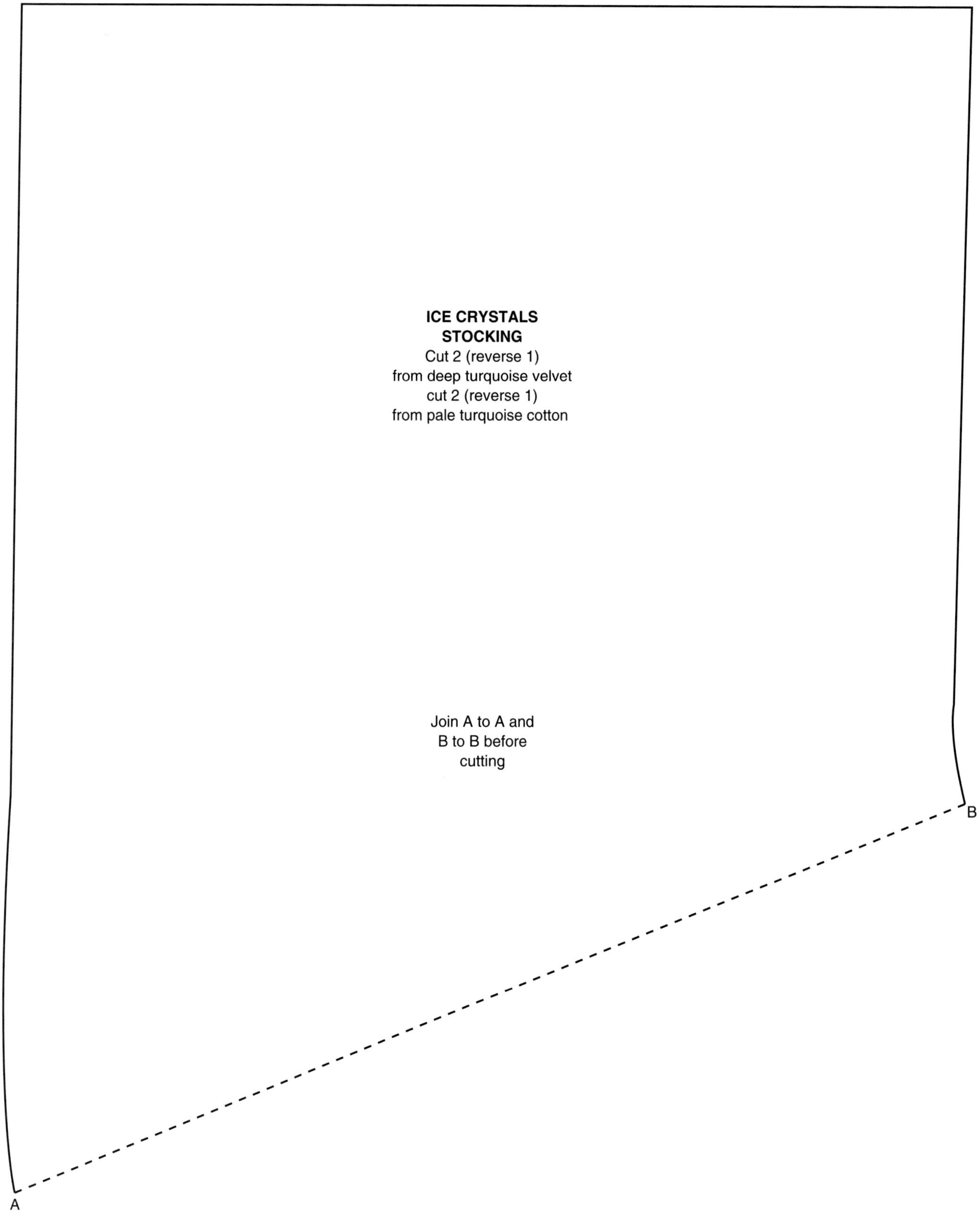

**ICE CRYSTALS
STOCKING**
Cut 2 (reverse 1)
from deep turquoise velvet
cut 2 (reverse 1)
from pale turquoise cotton

Join A to A and
B to B before
cutting

B

A

COLOR KEY

6-Strand Embroidery Floss	Yards
☐ White #1	15
▨ Pale turquoise #185	6
▨ Deep turquoise #189	12
Medium (#16) Braid	
■ Sky blue #014HL	6
▨ Light aqua #4639	13
● Attach dangle to cuff	

Color numbers given are for Coats & Clark Anchor 6-strand embroidery floss and Kreinik Medium (#16) Braid.

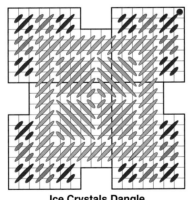

Ice Crystals Dangle
17 holes x 17 holes
Cut 3

A

Join A to A and
B to B before
cutting

B

Victorian Patchwork

*Patterned after a crazy quilt, this
eye-catching stocking will delight the
needlecrafter in your family!*

Skill Level: Intermediate

Materials
- 2 sheets 7-count soft plastic canvas
- Chenille yarn as listed in color key
- Heavy (#32) braid as listed in color key
- #16 tapestry needle
- 12" ⅞"-wide cream satin ribbon

Project Notes

Stocking back may be left unstitched or covered with felt or other fabric as desired, or it may be stitched in one of the yarn colors used on the front. Be sure to purchase extra yarn if planning to stitch the back.

If desired, twisted yarn cording may be substituted for hanger and may be sewn or glued inside cuff areas near seam.

When stitching, place needle very close to the end of the yarn. Chenille yarn tends to wear through and may need to be clipped off a few times while stitching. Some of the plush may be lost during stitching, but the yarn is quite full and this will not affect the finished appearance.

Instructions

1. Cut stocking pieces according to graph (page 116). Stocking back will remain unstitched.

2. Stitch holly berries and leaves on cuff following graph, then using mulberry and alphabet provided, center and Cross Stitch name in blue area, leaving one bar between letters. Fill in cuff background with sandstone Continental Stitches.

3. Stitch each patch below cuff following graph. Work Straight Stitches with gold braid when background stitching is completed.

4. Overcast top edge of stocking front with sandstone. Matching edges, Whipstitch front to back around sides and bottom with sandstone at cuff and with adjacent colors at remaining edges.

5. Thread one end of cream satin ribbon through stocking back at hole indicated on graph. Tie ends in a tight knot. Pull ribbon so knot is hidden inside stocking.

— Designed by Joan Green

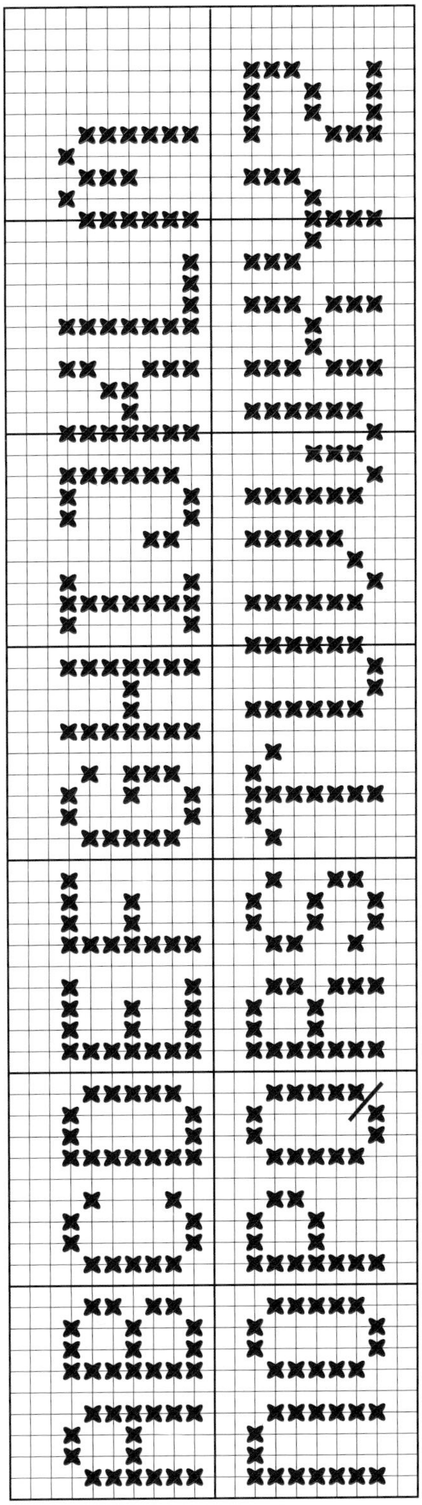

Alphabet

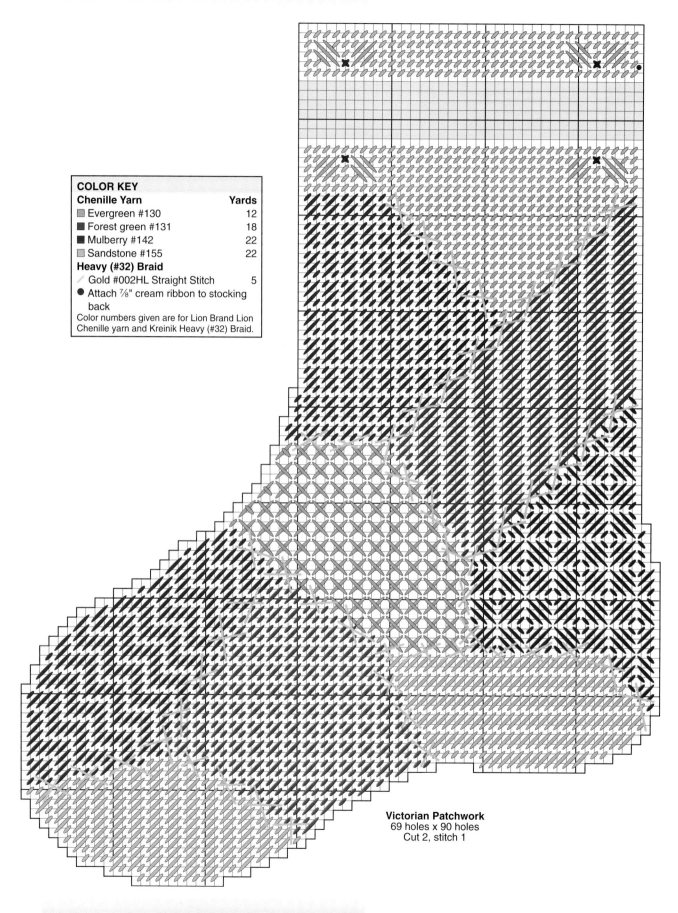

COLOR KEY

Chenille Yarn	Yards
▨ Evergreen #130	12
■ Forest green #131	18
■ Mulberry #142	22
▨ Sandstone #155	22

Heavy (#32) Braid

╱ Gold #002HL Straight Stitch	5
● Attach ⅞" cream ribbon to stocking back	

Color numbers given are for Lion Brand Lion Chenille yarn and Kreinik Heavy (#32) Braid.

Victorian Patchwork
69 holes x 90 holes
Cut 2, stitch 1

Skill Level: Beginner

Materials

- 2 sheets 7-count plastic canvas
- Plastic canvas yarn as listed in color key
- Heavy (#32) braid as listed in color key
- #16 tapestry needle
- ⅜" gold jingle bell
- ½" plastic ring

Instructions

1. Cut plastic canvas according to graph (page 118).

2. Stitch stocking front following graph with one strand yarn and two strands braid. Add French Knot for eye over completed background stitching. Using photo as a guide, sew jingle bell to end of cap with medium navy yarn.

3. For stocking back, reverse remaining stocking piece and Continental Stitch with medium navy.

4. Using emerald green throughout, Overcast top edges of stocking front and back. Matching edges, Whipstitch front to back.

5. Wrap plastic ring with emerald green yarn, then sew to top back corner of stocking.

— Designed by Lois Winston for Coats & Clark

Christmas Fun for Kids!

- Let your kids help you bake and decorate Christmas cookies.
- Help siblings wrap gifts for their brothers or sisters.
- Encourage kids to send Grandma and Grandpa a home-made card.

Father Christmas

What are the holidays without Father Christmas? Bearing gifts for all, he makes an attractive stocking for the man of the house.

COLOR KEY

Plastic Canvas Yarn	Yards
☐ White #01	2
▨ Flesh #248	2
▨ Nickel #401	2
▨ Honey gold #645	1
☐ Emerald green #676	5
▨ Paddy green #686	3
■ Bright red #901	5
■ Cardinal #917	2

Uncoded areas are medium
navy #860 Continental Stitches 60
● Medium navy #860 French Knot

Heavy (#32) Braid

☐ Gold #002HL	5
☐ Pearl #032	10

Color numbers given are for Coats & Clark
J. & P. Coats plastic canvas yarn and
Kreinik Heavy (#32) Braid.

Father Christmas
59 holes x 76 holes
Cut 2
Stitch 1 as graphed
Reverse 1, Continental
Stitch with medium navy

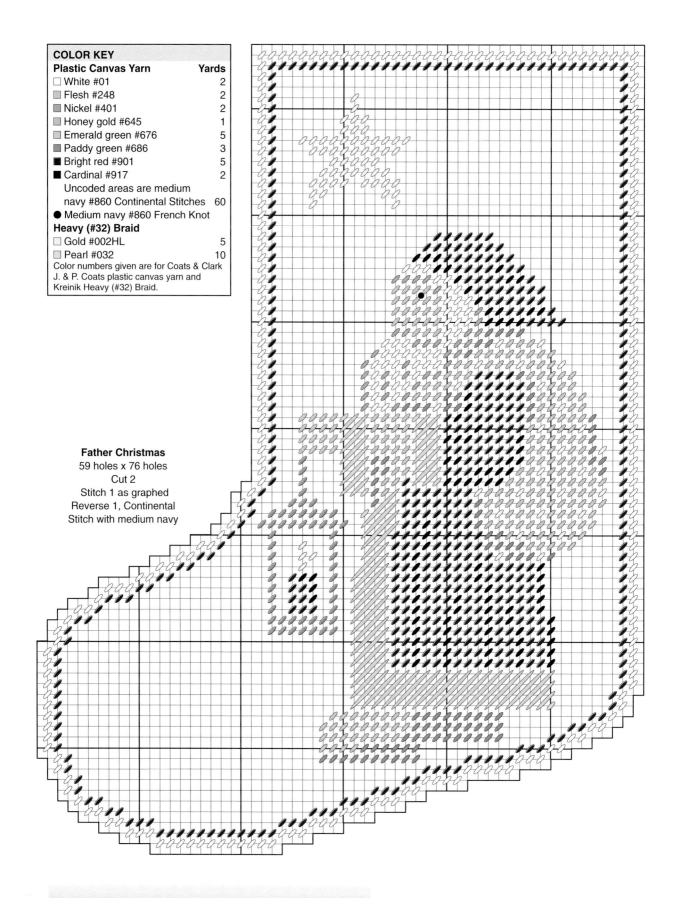

Elegant Desk Accessories

This beautiful box and bookmark set makes a wonderful stocking stuffer for use in a student's or work-at-home mom's office!

Pencil
Bright &
Hair He
Gingham
Mini Books
Critter Cadd
Camping Uter

Skill Level
Intermediate

Materials
- 1 sheet ivory 14-count plastic canvas
- 1/16" metallic ribbon as listed in color key
- Glass seed beads as listed in color key
- 1 yard 1"-wide polyester rayon ribbon: floral print #8650-13
- 2 yards 1/4"-wide Mylar cord: gold #2001-15
- #24 tapestry needle
- #10 crewel needle
- Ivory quilting thread
- 2" red rayon tassel
- Tacky craft glue

Project Notes
To work beaded areas, use quilting thread and crewel needle. Pour a few beads of each color into a shallow, rimmed container. Bring needle up at lower left of first stitch. Pick up bead with needle tip and attach bead with a Half Cross Stitch (from lower left to upper right).

Work horizontal rows from left to right and from right to left, with all Half Cross Stitches slanting the same direction. Work vertical and diagonal rows from top to bottom. If any beads appear to be loose, stitch through them a second time. To straighten a long row of beads, run needle back through entire line after completing it.

When working with metallic ribbon, keep ribbon smooth and flat. To prevent twisting and tangling, guide ribbon between thumb and forefinger of free hand. Drop needle occasionally to let ribbon unwind.

Bookmark
1. Cut plastic canvas according to graphs (at right).

2. Following Project Notes, work beaded portion of designs first.

3. Thread tapestry needle with 18" length of metallic ribbon and work remainder of design using Slanting Gobelin Stitches, Half Cross Stitches and Cross Stitches.

4. Cut floral print ribbon 1" longer than bookmark; fold over 1/2" at each short end. With quilting thread, attach edges of ribbon to center of plastic canvas with tiny stitches.

5. Cut two pieces of Mylar cord the same length as bookmark. Glue along side edges of floral print ribbon (see photo).

6. Using gold ribbon throughout, Overcast bookmark, then Whipstitch wrong sides of medallion together. Attach one corner of medallion to center top of bookmark; attach red tassel to center bottom.

Trinket Box
1. Cut plastic canvas according to graphs (pages 121 and 122). Cut one 44-hole x 44-hole piece for box bottom. Box bottom will remain unstitched.

2. Following Project Notes, work beaded portion of designs first.

3. Thread tapestry needle with 18" length of metallic ribbon and work remainder of design using Slanting Gobelin Stitches, Half Cross Stitches and Cross Stitches.

4. Following step 4 for bookmark, cut, then crisscross and attach two pieces of floral print ribbon at center of lid top. Cut and glue Mylar cord along edges of floral print ribbon.

5. Using gold ribbon throughout, Whipstitch lid sides together, matching colors at corners.

Whipstitch sides to top, again matching colors at corners. Overcast bottom edges of lid sides.

6. With gold ribbon, Whipstitch box sides together and then sides to box bottom.

7. Cut floral print ribbon 1" longer than circumference of box. Fold ribbon under at each short end and run ribbon strip around box between beading and stitching designs, attaching ribbon to plastic canvas with quilting thread. Whipstitch folded ribbon edges together with quilting thread.

8. Cut and glue Mylar cord around box along top and bottom edges of floral print ribbon.

— Designed by Carol Krob

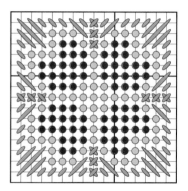

Bookmark Medallion A
16 holes x 16 holes
Cut 1

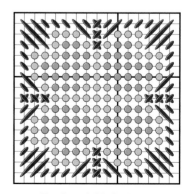

Bookmark Medallion B
16 holes x 16 holes
Cut 1

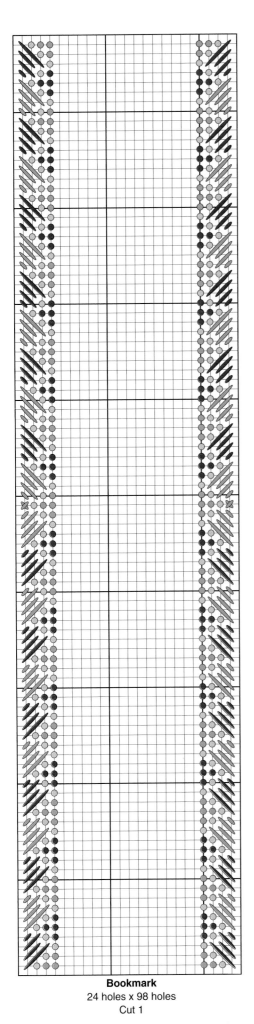

Bookmark
24 holes x 98 holes
Cut 1

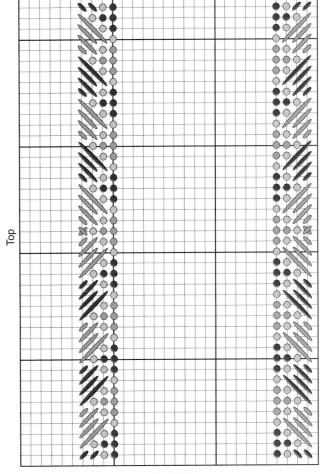

Box Side
29 holes x 44 holes
Cut 4

Top

COLOR KEY

⅟₁₆ " **Metallic Ribbon**	**Reels**
◼ Aquamarine #684	2
◼ Red #003HL	2
◻ Gold #002HL	2
Glass Seed Beads	**Packages**
● Sea breeze #2008	1
○ Victorian gold #2011	2
● Red red #2013	1

Color numbers given are for Kreinik ⅟₁₆ "
Ribbon and Mill Hill glass seed beads.

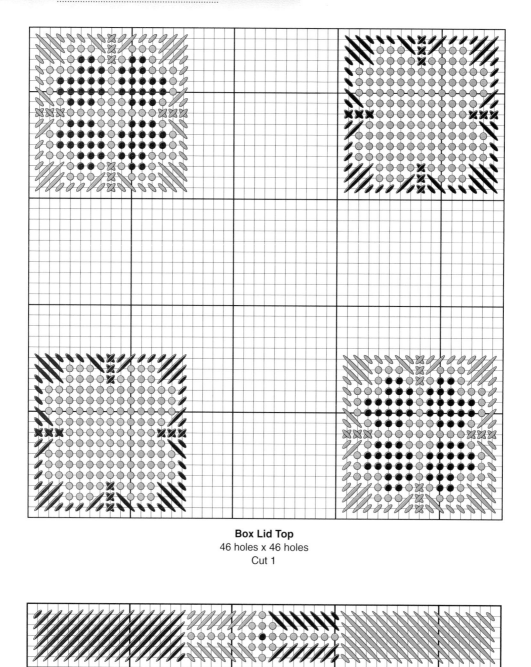

Box Lid Top
46 holes x 46 holes
Cut 1

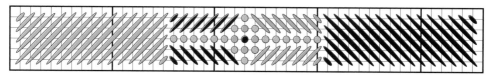

Box Lid Side A
46 holes x 6 holes
Cut 2

Box Lid Side B
46 holes x 6 holes
Cut 2

Gifts for the Bookworm

Three attractive bookmarks make cherished gifts that will see much use throughout the year!

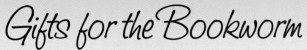

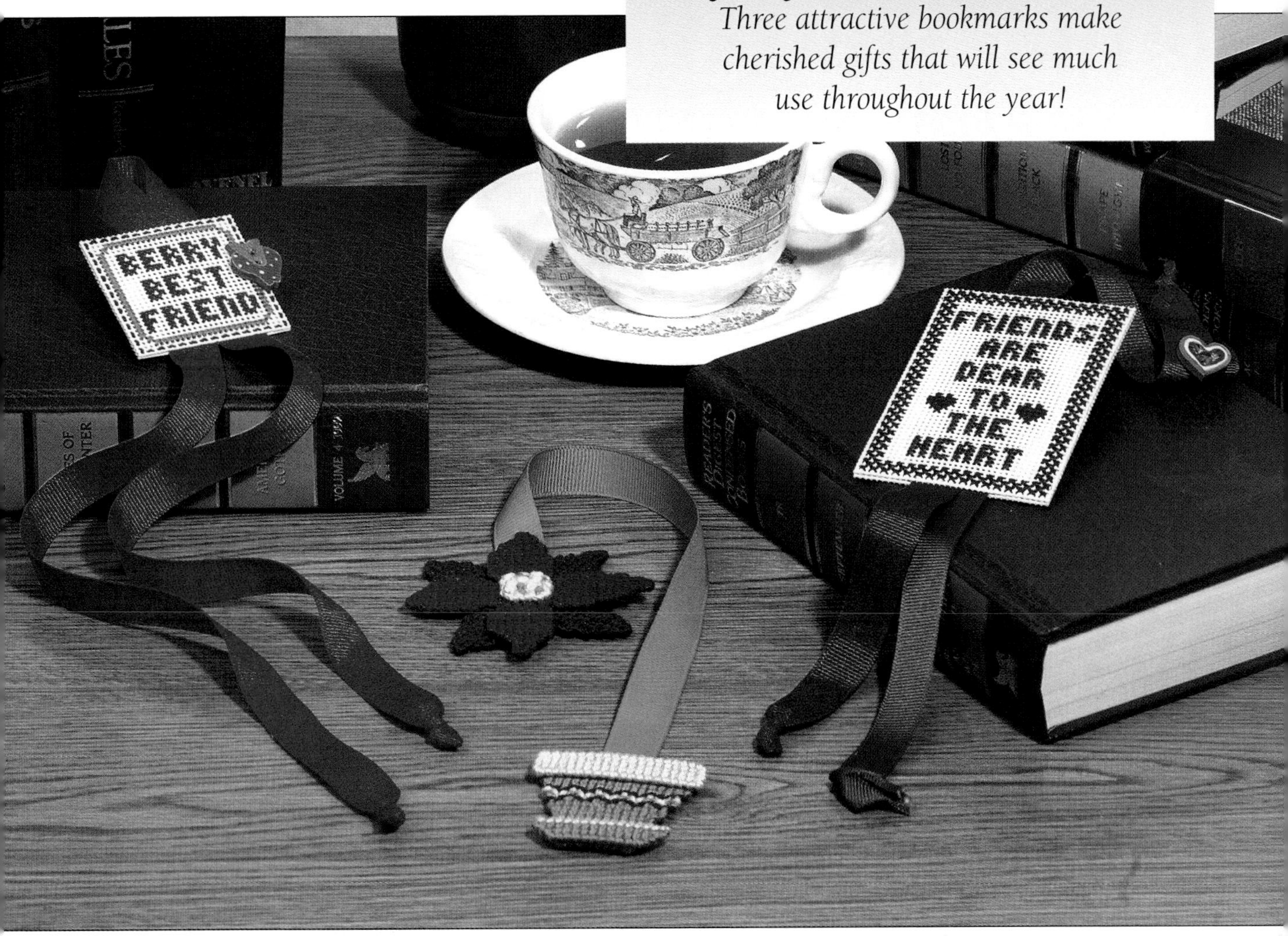

Potted Poinsettia

Skill Level: Beginner

Materials

- ¼ sheet 10-count plastic canvas
- #3 pearl cotton as listed in color key
- ⅓ yard ⅝"-wide green grosgrain ribbon
- High-temperature glue gun

Instructions

1. Cut plastic canvas according to graphs (page 125).

2. Stitch pieces following graphs, stitching one poinsettia with Christmas red and one with garnet. Overcast poinsettia center and top edge of pot saucer with topaz; Overcast side and bottom edges of saucer with bright Christmas green. Overcast remaining pieces with adjacent colors.

3. Add French Knots and Backstitches last, making sure to Backstitch over edges of pot.

4. Glue wrong side of red poinsettia to right side of garnet poinsettia, evenly spacing red leaves between garnet leaves. Glue center to top middle of flower. Glue rim to top edge of pot and saucer to bottom edge.

5. Cut ribbon to desired length, then glue ends to backs of flower and pot.

—Designed by Celia Lange Designs

Berry Best Friend

Skill Level: Beginner

Materials

- ¼ sheet 14-count ivory plastic canvas
- 6-strand embroidery floss as listed in color key
- ¾ yard ⅝"-wide grosgrain ribbon: hot red #252
- Ceramic strawberry button #86079
- Green sewing thread to match leaves in button
- #24 tapestry needle

Instructions

1. Cut plastic canvas according to graph (page 125).

2. Using 4 strands floss, Cross Stitch letters and dark pistachio green border following graph on front piece only. Back piece will remain unstitched.

3. Sew button to front piece where indicated on graph.

4. Tie each ribbon end in a knot. Find center point of ribbon and crisscross ribbon, making a loop. Following graph for ribbon placement and using photo as a guide, place ribbon, with loop at top, between front and back pieces, making sure ribbon lies flat between pieces.

5. Following graph, join front and back together on all four sides with a Running Stitch, except at button attachment where Running Stitch will be on backside only.

— Designed by Linda Wyszynski

Friends Are Dear to the Heart

Skill Level: Beginner

Materials
- ¼ sheet 14-count ivory plastic canvas
- 6-strand embroidery floss as listed in color key
- Ribbon floss as listed in color key
- ½ yard each ⅝"-wide grosgrain ribbon: hot red #252, forest green #587
- Ceramic heart button #86078
- Red sewing thread to match red in button
- Ecru sewing thread
- #24 tapestry needle

Instructions

1. Cut plastic canvas according to graph (at right).

2. Using ribbon floss and 4 strands embroidery floss, Cross Stitch letters, hearts and border following graph on front piece only. Back piece will remain unstitched.

3. Tie each end of grosgrain ribbon in a knot. Overlap ribbon, placing red on top. Following

graph for ribbon placement and using photo as a guide, center and place ribbon between front and back pieces, making sure ribbon lies flat between pieces.

4. Following graph, join front and back together on all four sides with 2 strands ecru.

5. With ribbons lying flat and with red sewing thread, sew button to center of overlapped ribbon 3" from top knot.

— Designed by Linda Wyszynski

COLOR KEY
FRIENDS ARE DEAR TO THE HEART

6-Strand Embroidery Floss	Yards
■ Ultra dark pistachio green #890	6
Ribbon Floss	
■ Red #142-12	4
Sewing Thread	
⁄ Ecru	
▬ Ribbon placement	

Color numbers given are for DMC 6-strand embroidery floss and Rhode Island Textile RibbonFloss.

Friends Are Dear to the Heart
34 holes x 52 holes
Cut 2, stitch 1

Berry Best Friend
28 holes x 28 holes
Cut 2, stitch 1

COLOR KEY
BERRY BEST FRIEND

6-Strand Embroidery Floss	Yards
■ Ultra deep rose #326	3
▨ Dark pistachio green #367	2
● Attach button	
— Ribbon placement	

Color numbers given are for DMC 6-strand embroidery floss.

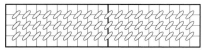

Pot Rim
19 holes x 4 holes
Cut 1

Pot Saucer
15 holes x 3 holes
Cut 1

COLOR KEY
POTTED POINSETTIA

#3 Pearl Cotton	Yards
■ Christmas red #321	5
▨ Bright Christmas green #700	4
Medium garnet #815	4
▢ Topaz #725	2
● Lemon #300 French Knot	1
╱ Christmas red #321 Backstitch	
╱ Topaz #725 Backstitch	

Color numbers given are for DMC #3 pearl cotton.

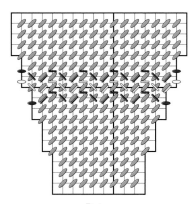

Pot
17 holes x 17 holes
Cut 1

Poinsettia Center
6 holes x 6 holes
Cut 1

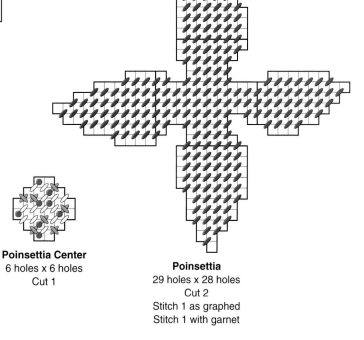

Poinsettia
29 holes x 28 holes
Cut 2
Stitch 1 as graphed
Stitch 1 with garnet

Mini Stocking Ornament

Stitch this sweet ornament for your Christmas tree. Or, hang it in its own special spot with your other stockings!

Skill Level: Advanced beginner

Materials

- ¼ sheet 7-count plastic canvas
- Plastic canvas yarn as listed in color key
- #16 tapestry needle
- 1½" brown flocked Santa bear
- Pencil
- Hot-glue gun

Instructions

1. Cut plastic canvas according to graphs.

2. Stitch pieces following graphs. Keep Turkey Loops a consistent length by forming loops around a pencil.

3. Overcast holly sprigs and spears with holly yarn and top edges of stockings with white. Whipstitch wrong sides of stocking together with adjacent colors.

4. For hanger, thread a 6" length of white yarn through top back corner hole on stocking back cuff. Tie ends in a knot, trimming as necessary.

5. Using photo as a guide, glue Santa bear just inside top of stocking; glue one holly spear on each side of bear. Glue holly sprig to heel of stocking front.

— *Designed by Angie Arickx*

Stocking Back
18 holes x 19 holes
Cut 1

Holly Spear
5 holes x 8 holes
Cut 2

Holly Sprig
5 holes x 8 holes
Cut 1

Stocking Front
18 holes x 19 holes
Cut 1

COLOR KEY

Plastic Canvas Yarn	Yards
■ Christmas red #02	5
▨ Holly #27	2
● Christmas red #02 French Knot	
○ White #41 Turkey Loop	

Color numbers given are for Uniek Needloft plastic canvas yarn.

Quick & Easy Gifts

Running out of shopping days before Christmas? Why not make any of these appealing and handy gifts for friends and family!

Snowman Plant Poke

Skill Level: Beginner

Materials
- ¼ sheet 7-count plastic canvas
- Worsted weight yarn as listed in color key
- 8" ⅜"-diameter dowel
- 2 small pieces twig
- High-temperature glue gun

Instructions

1. Cut plastic canvas according to graphs (page 128).

2. Continental Stitch pieces following graphs. Overcast hat with black, vest area on snowman with country red and remaining edges with white.

3. Add French Knots and paddy green Backstitches last, making sure to Backstitch over vest edges where indicated on graph.

4. Using photo as a guide, glue hat at an angle to snowman's head; glue twigs (for arms) to backside of upper body. Glue dowel to backside of lower body.

— Designed by Celia Lange Designs

Festive Sachets

Skill Level: Beginner

Materials
- ¼ sheet 10-count plastic canvas
- Ribbon floss as listed in color key
- Metallic ribbon floss as listed in color key
- Nylon thread
- Scented potpourri or 4 cosmetic puffs sprayed with perfume

Instructions

1. Cut plastic canvas according to graphs (page 133).

2. Stitch pieces following graphs. Overcast inside and outside edges of the Cheers cutout border with red. Overcast inside and outside edges of the Joy cutout border with grass green.

3. With wrong sides together and using grass green, Whipstitch Cheers back and front together where indicated on graph, filling with potpourri or two perfumed cosmetic puffs before closing.

4. Repeat step 3 for Joy sachet using red ribbon floss.

5. For Cheers sachet, cut two 12" lengths of grass green ribbon floss. Combine lengths and tie in a bow. With nylon thread, tack bow to center top of border.

6. Repeat step 5 for Joy sachet using red ribbon floss.

— Designed by Mary T. Cosgrove

Mom & Dad Key Rings

Skill Level: Beginner

Materials

- ¼ sheet 10-count plastic canvas
- Ribbon floss as listed in color key
- Metallic ribbon floss as listed in color key
- 2 (24mm) gold split key rings

Instructions

1. Cut plastic canvas according to graphs (page 129).

2. Cross Stitch letters with opal following graphs. Continental Stitch backgrounds using a double strand of ribbon floss. Add Backstitches over completed background stitching using one strand ribbon floss.

3. Using two stitches of gold per hole throughout, Overcast center strip of each piece. Fold each key ring at center strip so wrong sides are together and edges match. Whipstitch front and back squares together. **Note:** *Don't Whipstitch center strip together.*

4. Add one gold key ring at fold of each stitched piece.

— Designed by Mary T. Cosgrove

Candy Canes Magnet

Skill Level: Beginner

Materials

- Small piece 7-count plastic canvas
- Plastic canvas yarn as listed in color key
- 8" ⅜"-wide green plaid ribbon
- ½" round magnet
- Hot-glue gun

Instructions

1. Cut plastic canvas according to graphs (below right).

2. Continental Stitch pieces following graphs. Overcast with white.

3. Wrap red yarn around each candy cane where indicated on graph.

4. Using photo as a guide, cross candy canes in center and glue in place. Wrap ribbon around candy canes and tie in a bow. Glue magnet on back.

— Designed by Kathleen Kennebeck

COLOR KEY
SNOWMAN PLANT POKE

Worsted Weight Yarn	Yards
☐ White #1	8
■ Black #12	2
▨ Paddy green #686	1
■ Country red #914	2
● Black #12 French Knot	
╱ Paddy green #686 Backstitch	
● Country red #914 French Knot	
Color numbers given are for Coats & Clark Red Heart Classic Yarn.	

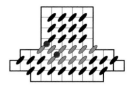

Snowman Hat
11 holes x 7 holes
Cut 1

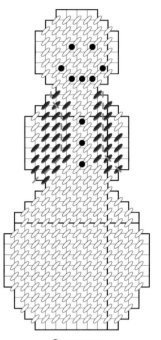

Snowman
14 holes x 30 holes
Cut 1

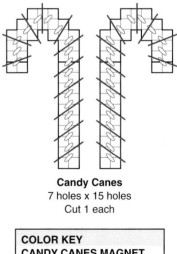

Candy Canes
7 holes x 15 holes
Cut 1 each

COLOR KEY
CANDY CANES MAGNET

Plastic Canvas Yarn	Yards
■ Red #02	1
☐ White #41	1½
Color numbers given are for Uniek Needloft plastic canvas yarn.	

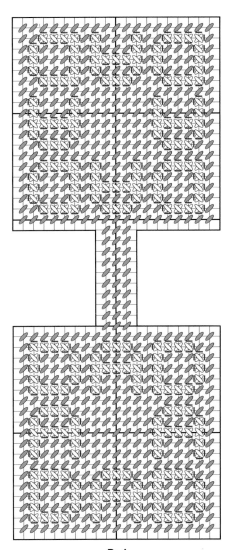

Dad
20 holes x 49 holes
Cut 1

COLOR KEY
MOM & DAD KEY RINGS

Ribbon Floss	Yards
▨ Grass green #142F-9	26
■ Red #142F-12	24

Metallic Ribbon Floss

☐ Opal #144F-10	20
Gold #144-1 Overcasting	4

Color numbers given are for Rhode Island Textile RibbonFloss and metallic RibbonFloss.

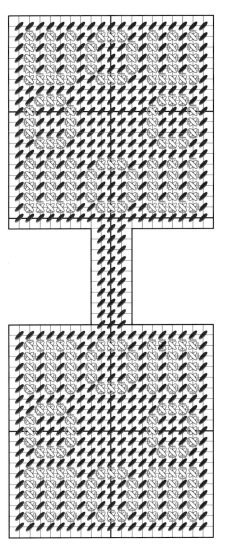

Mom
20 holes x 49 holes
Cut 1

Graphs continued on page 133

Festive Jewelry
*As fun to make as they are
to wear during the holidays!*

Gingerbread Barrette

Skill Level: Beginner

Materials

- ¼ sheet 10-count plastic canvas
- #3 pearl cotton as listed in color key
- 2¾" barrette back
- High-temperature glue gun

Instructions

1. Cut plastic canvas according to graphs (page 131).

2. Continental Stitch pieces following graphs. Overcast gingerbread man and hearts with white and barrette with Christmas red. Add French Knots and Backstitches last.

3. Thread a 3" length of Christmas red from front to back where indicated on gingerbread man graph with green dots. Tie in a small bow, trimming ends as necessary. Glue ends to gingerbread man front.

4. Glue base to barrette. Using photo as a guide, glue ginger-

Barrette Base
31 holes x 4 holes
Cut 1

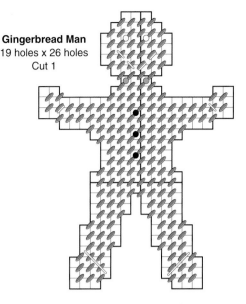

Gingerbread Man
19 holes x 26 holes
Cut 1

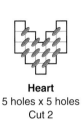

Heart
5 holes x 5 holes
Cut 2

COLOR KEY	
GINGERBREAD BARRETTE	
#3 Pearl Cotton	**Yards**
■ Christmas red #321	2
▨ Russet #434	4
⁄ White Backstitch	3
○ White French Knot	
● Very dark mocha brown #838	
French Knot	1
Color numbers given are for DMC #3 pearl cotton.	

bread man to center of barrette, then glue one heart to each side of gingerbread man near ends of barrette.

— *Designed by Celia Lange Designs*

Jingle Bell Pull Pin

Skill Level: Beginner

Materials
- Scrap piece 14-count plastic canvas
- #5 pearl cotton as listed in color key
- ¹⁄₁₆"-wide metallic ribbon as listed in color key
- 6½" ⅜"-wide gold-edged red satin ribbon
- 1" pin back
- 4 (6mm) gold jingle bells
- High-temperature glue gun

Instructions
1. Cut plastic canvas according to graphs (page 132).

2. Continental Stitch pieces following graphs. Overcast bell pull with Christmas red and holly with bright Christmas green. Add gold Backstitches last, stitching bells in while Backstitching.

3. Glue pin back to backside of stitched bell pull. Using photo as

a guide, glue both pieces of holly to center top front of bell pull.

4. Tie ribbon in a bow and trim ends in an inverted V. Center and glue bow just beneath holly leaves, rippling streamers down sides of bell pull.

— *Designed by Celia Lange Designs*

Topiary Tree Pin

Skill Level: Beginner

Materials
- ¼ sheet 10-count clear plastic canvas
- Small piece 10-count white plastic canvas
- #3 pearl cotton as listed in color key
- ¾" pin back
- High-temperature glue gun

Instructions
1. Cut one tree from clear plastic canvas and one star from white plastic canvas according to graphs (page 132). Star will remain unstitched.

2. Stitch tree following graph. Overcast green portion of tree with kelly green and remainder of tree piece with adjacent colors. Backstitch with white last, making sure to Backstitch over

pot edges where indicated on graph.

3. With lemon, Cross Stitch star to top of tree.

4. Glue pin back to backside of stitched piece.

— *Designed by Celia Lange Designs*

Stocking Earrings

Skill Level: Advanced beginner

Materials
- Small piece 14-count plastic canvas
- 6-strand embroidery floss as listed in color key
- Fine (#8) braid as listed in color key
- Glossy thread as listed in color key
- 1 yard ¹⁄₁₆" metallic ribbon: red #003
- #22 tapestry needle
- Glass seed beads as listed in color key
- Antique glass seed beads as listed in color key
- Beading needle
- Red and white sewing thread
- 2" x 4" piece red felt
- Fishhook ear wires
- Tacky craft glue

Project Notes
Work beaded areas with doubled

sewing thread and Half Cross Stitches going in the same direction.

When working with metallic ribbon or braid, keep ribbon and braid smooth and flat. To prevent twisting and tangling, guide ribbon and braid between thumb and forefinger of free hand. Drop needle occasionally to let ribbon and braid unwind.

Instructions

1. Cut plastic canvas according to graph (below).

2. Stitch stockings following graph, using 3 strands embroidery floss. Add beads, using white sewing thread for white beads and red sewing thread for red beads.

3. Overcast cuff areas with white glossy thread. Overcast stockings with 1/16" red metallic ribbon, stitching two to three times at corners as need-

ed for coverage.

4. Sew a 1/4" loop of forest green braid at top back corner of each stocking.

5. Cut two pieces felt to fit stockings. Apply a thin layer of glue to felt and pat lightly into position on backside of each stocking. Allow to dry.

6. Attach ear wires to green loops.

— *Designed by Judi Kauffman for DMC*

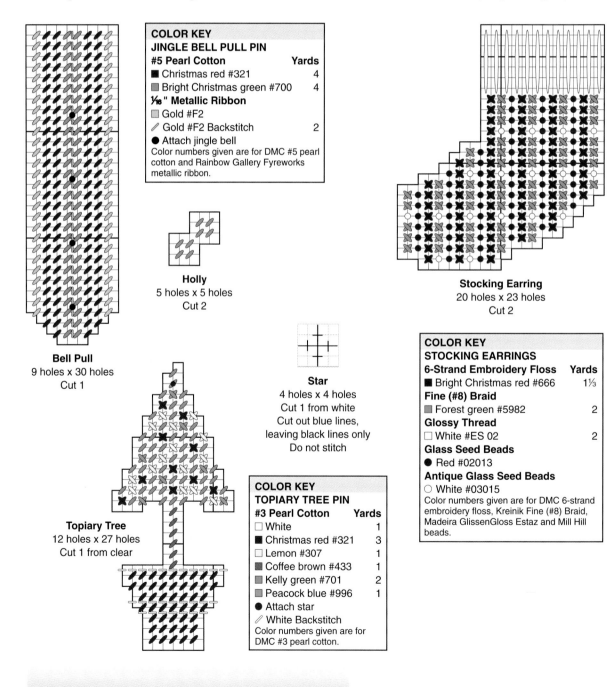

COLOR KEY
JINGLE BELL PULL PIN

#5 Pearl Cotton	Yards
■ Christmas red #321	4
■ Bright Christmas green #700	4

1/16" Metallic Ribbon

□ Gold #F2	
╱ Gold #F2 Backstitch	2
● Attach jingle bell	

Color numbers given are for DMC #5 pearl cotton and Rainbow Gallery Fyreworks metallic ribbon.

Holly
5 holes x 5 holes
Cut 2

Bell Pull
9 holes x 30 holes
Cut 1

Star
4 holes x 4 holes
Cut 1 from white
Cut out blue lines,
leaving black lines only
Do not stitch

Topiary Tree
12 holes x 27 holes
Cut 1 from clear

COLOR KEY
TOPIARY TREE PIN

#3 Pearl Cotton	Yards
□ White	1
■ Christmas red #321	3
□ Lemon #307	1
■ Coffee brown #433	1
■ Kelly green #701	2
■ Peacock blue #996	1
● Attach star	
╱ White Backstitch	

Color numbers given are for DMC #3 pearl cotton.

Stocking Earring
20 holes x 23 holes
Cut 2

COLOR KEY
STOCKING EARRINGS

6-Strand Embroidery Floss	Yards
■ Bright Christmas red #666	1 1/3

Fine (#8) Braid

■ Forest green #5982	2

Glossy Thread

□ White #ES 02	2

Glass Seed Beads

● Red #02013	

Antique Glass Seed Beads

○ White #03015	

Color numbers given are for DMC 6-strand embroidery floss, Kreinik Fine (#8) Braid, Madeira GlissenGloss Estaz and Mill Hill beads.

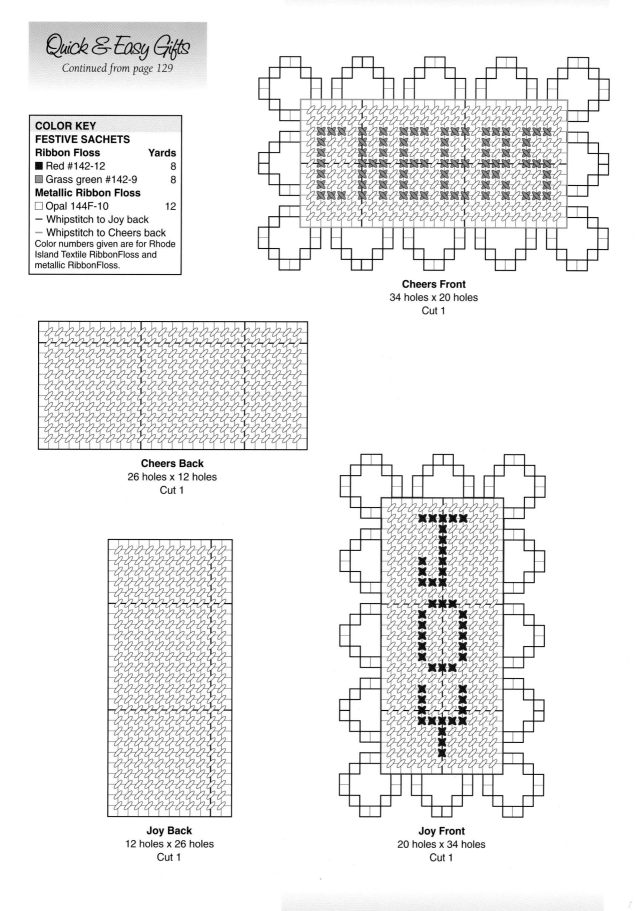

Quick & Easy Gifts
Continued from page 129

COLOR KEY
FESTIVE SACHETS

Ribbon Floss	Yards
■ Red #142-12	8
▨ Grass green #142-9	8

Metallic Ribbon Floss

☐ Opal 144F-10	12

− Whipstitch to Joy back
− Whipstitch to Cheers back

Color numbers given are for Rhode Island Textile RibbonFloss and metallic RibbonFloss.

Cheers Front
34 holes x 20 holes
Cut 1

Cheers Back
26 holes x 12 holes
Cut 1

Joy Back
12 holes x 26 holes
Cut 1

Joy Front
20 holes x 34 holes
Cut 1

Santa & Friends

What is Christmas without Santa Claus?
Be sure to stitch at least one cheerful
Santa to add to your Christmas decor.
Santa's friends, including wintry
snowmen and sweet angels, make
delightful holiday accents too!

Folk-Art Santa & Angel

Showcase your plastic canvas stitching skills by creating this striking Santa and Angel duo to display this holiday season.

Old-World Santa

Skill Level: Advanced

Materials
- 1 sheet 7-count plastic canvas
- 1 sheet 7-count soft plastic canvas
- Plastic canvas cotton yarn as listed in color key
- ⅛" metallic ribbon as listed in color key
- 3 yards gold cord
- Small amount white 6-strand embroidery floss
- 3 (40mm) star crystals #6211P
- 3 (9mm x 31mm) drop crystals #6221P
- 1¼" off-white pompon
- Large-curl white doll hair
- Small-curl white doll hair
- Bamboo skewer
- Polyester fiberfill
- Craft glue

Head & Nose

1. Cut head and nose from soft plastic canvas according to graphs (pages 140 and 141).

2. Stitch head following graph, overlapping where indicated on graph before stitching is completed. Backstitch eyes with 6 strands white floss over completed Smyrna Crosses.

3. With pale peach, Whipstitch longest straight edges of nose pieces together, Overcasting remaining edges. With same piece of yarn used for Overcasting, attach nose to face between eyes and cheeks, spreading nose slightly.

4. With pale peach, Whipstitch darts at top and bottom of head together, lightly stuffing head with fiberfill before closing.

5. Glue large-curl hair to back, sides and top of head as desired, following manufacturer's directions.

Robe, Sleeves & Hat

1. Cut hat and sleeve pieces from soft plastic canvas; cut robe panels and robe base from regular plastic canvas according to graphs (pages 140–143). Robe base will remain unstitched.

2. Stitch pieces following graphs, overlapping hat where indicated on graph before stitching is completed. Overcast bottom edges of hat and top edges of robe panels with off-white.

3. Whipstitch robe panels together with adjacent colors. Backstitch with gold ribbon over Whipstitching. Lightly stuff Santa robe with fiberfill, then Whipstitch base to bottom of robe with off-white.

4. With rose red, Whipstitch darts at top of hat together. Attach pompon to point of hat with off-white yarn.

5. Matching dots, Whipstitch one each of sleeves A and B to one gusset down front of sleeve with adjacent colors. Whipstitch back edges of sleeve together with adjacent colors. Repeat with remaining sleeve pieces.

6. Overcast bottom edges of sleeves with off-white. Backstitch with gold ribbon over Whipstitching.

Hands & Staff

1. Cut hands and staff from soft plastic canvas according to graphs (page 141).

2. Stitch hands with sage and staff with caramel following graphs.

3. Overcast short ends of staff with caramel. Cut six varying lengths (5"–12") of gold cord. Thread crystals on cord, then thread cord to wrong side of staff at one short end.

4. Cut bamboo skewer slightly

shorter than staff, wrap staff around skewer and Whipstitch long edges together with caramel.

5. With wrong sides together, Whipstitch one hand A and one hand B together with sage.

6. With wrong sides together, Whipstitch remaining hands A and B together from one red dot around wrist to other red dot. Whipstitch front of hands A and B together from blue dot to blue dot. Overcast remaining edges.

7. Slip staff through opening in hand so that crystals hang from the top.

Beard & Mustache

1. Cut beard and mustache from regular plastic canvas according to graphs (pages 139 and 140).

2. Stitch pieces following graphs, Overcasting with white.

3. Glue large-curl hair as desired to beard and small-curl hair as desired to mustache following manufacturer's directions.

Assembly

1. Using photo as a guide, slip neck through top opening in robe and glue in place. Glue mustache and beard to head.

2. Glue hands inside sleeves, then glue arms to robe sides.

3. Place hat on head.

Angel

Skill Level: Advanced

Materials
- ½ sheet 7-count stiff plastic canvas
- 1½ sheets 7-count soft plastic canvas
- Plastic canvas cotton yarn as listed in color key
- Plastic canvas acrylic yarn as listed in color key
- Pearlized metallic cord as listed in color key

- ⅛" metallic ribbon as listed in color key
- 6-strand embroidery floss as listed in color key
- 2 (8mm x 4mm) ruby navette faceted stones
- 12mm x 6mm ruby navette faceted stone
- Brown curly doll hair
- 1⅓ yards ⅛"-wide red ribbon
- 10" ⅝"-wide white ribbon
- 5" ½"-wide pre-gathered white lace
- Bouquet red silk flowers
- Polyester fiberfill
- Craft glue

Head & Nose

1. Cut head and nose from soft plastic canvas according to graphs (page 139).

2. Stitch head following graph, overlapping before stitching is completed. Add highlights of eyes with white floss over completed stitching.

3. With pale peach, Whipstitch longest straight edges of nose pieces together, Overcasting remaining edges. With same piece of yarn used for Overcasting, attach nose to face between eyes and cheeks, spreading nose slightly.

4. Whipstitch darts at bottom of head together with pale peach. Whipstitch darts at top of head together with medium brown, lightly stuffing head with fiberfill before closing.

Dress, Sleeves & Hands

1. Cut dress pieces, sleeve pieces and hands from soft plastic canvas according to graphs (pages 138–142).

2. Stitch pieces following graphs. Overcast bottom edges of skirt panels, outer sleeves and inner sleeves with gold. Overcast

hands with pale peach.

3. With white, Overcast inside edges (neck opening) of dress top; matching dots, join top edges of dress sides to shoulder edges of dress top.

4. Whipstitch darts together at tops of skirt front and back panels with white. Whipstitch sides of skirt panels together with adjacent colors, placing two side panels between front and back panels. With white, Whipstitch top edge of skirt to bottom edge of dress top.

5. With white, Whipstitch elbow darts of outer sleeves together; Whipstitch top darts of outer sleeves together where indicated with arrow, then Whipstitch darts on both sides of center top dart together.

6. Matching dots, Whipstitch inner sleeves to outer sleeves with adjacent colors. Overcast remaining edges with white.

7. Using photo as a guide, glue hands inside sleeves, then glue shoulders of sleeves to dress sides.

Halo & Wings

1. Cut halo from soft plastic canvas and wings from stiff plastic canvas according to graphs (pages 140 and 143).

2. Stitch pieces following graphs, overlapping halo before stitching is completed.

3. Overcast edges of halo and wings with gold.

Finishing

1. Wrap white ribbon around waist, overlapping ends and trimming as necessary; glue in place. Glue lace to inner neck edge, overlapping ends at back. Trim as necessary.

2. Using photo as a guide, glue large faceted stone to front of

dress at neck; glue one small stone on each side of large stone.

3. Cut red ribbon into eight 6" lengths. Thread ribbon from back to front through holes indicated on graph. Tie in a bow, trimming ends as desired.

4. Following manufacturer's directions, glue hair to medium brown area of head.

5. Slip neck of head through neck opening on dress and glue in place. Center and glue wings to angel's back. Glue bouquet to hands. Place halo on head.

—Designed by Darla J. Fanton

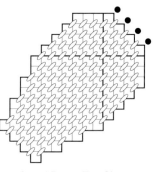

Angel Dress Top Side
14 holes x 14 holes
Cut 2 from soft

COLOR KEY	
ANGEL	
Plastic Canvas Cotton Yarn	**Yards**
☐ Pale peach #0109	10
■ Medium brown #0112	10
▨ Periwinkle #0129	1
▨ Old rose #0150	1
✑ Red #0153 Backstitch	1
Plastic Canvas Acrylic Yarn	
☐ White #0001	65
Pearlized Metallic Cord	
☐ White #3410-01	12
⅛" Metallic Ribbon	
☐ Gold #002HL	14
■ Star pink #092	4
6-Strand Embroidery Floss	
✑ White Backstitch	
● Attach red bows	
Color numbers given are for Spinrite acrylic plastic canvas yarn and Bernat cotton plastic canvas yarn, Darice Bright Pearls metallic cord and Kreinik /•" Ribbon.	

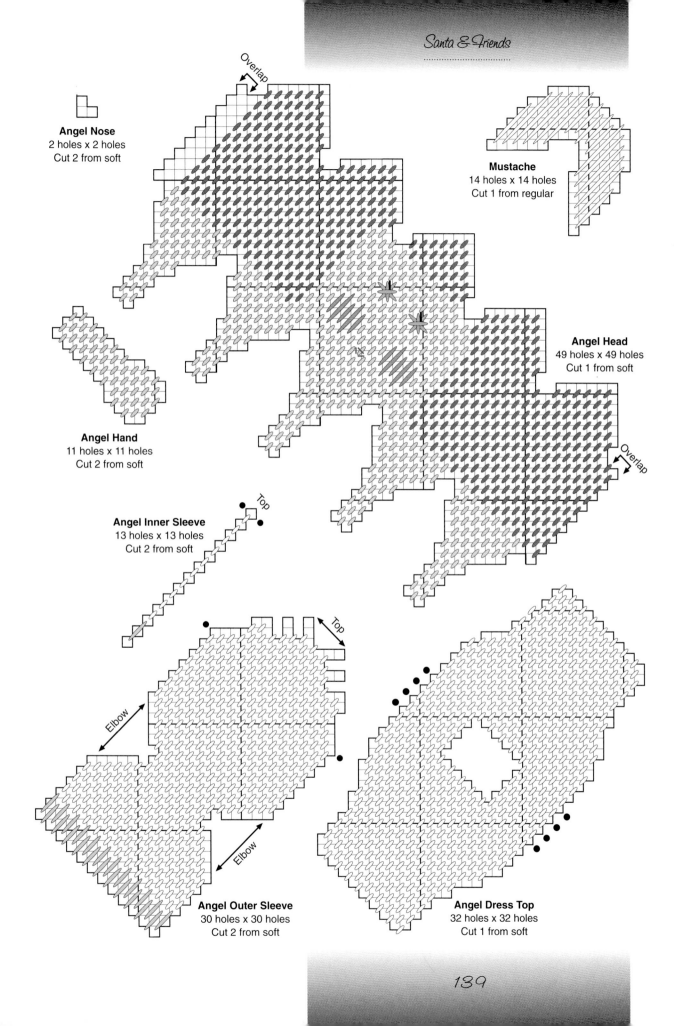

Angel Nose
2 holes x 2 holes
Cut 2 from soft

Overlap

Mustache
14 holes x 14 holes
Cut 1 from regular

Angel Head
49 holes x 49 holes
Cut 1 from soft

Overlap

Angel Hand
11 holes x 11 holes
Cut 2 from soft

Angel Inner Sleeve
13 holes x 13 holes
Cut 2 from soft

Top

Top

Elbow

Elbow

Angel Outer Sleeve
30 holes x 30 holes
Cut 2 from soft

Angel Dress Top
32 holes x 32 holes
Cut 1 from soft

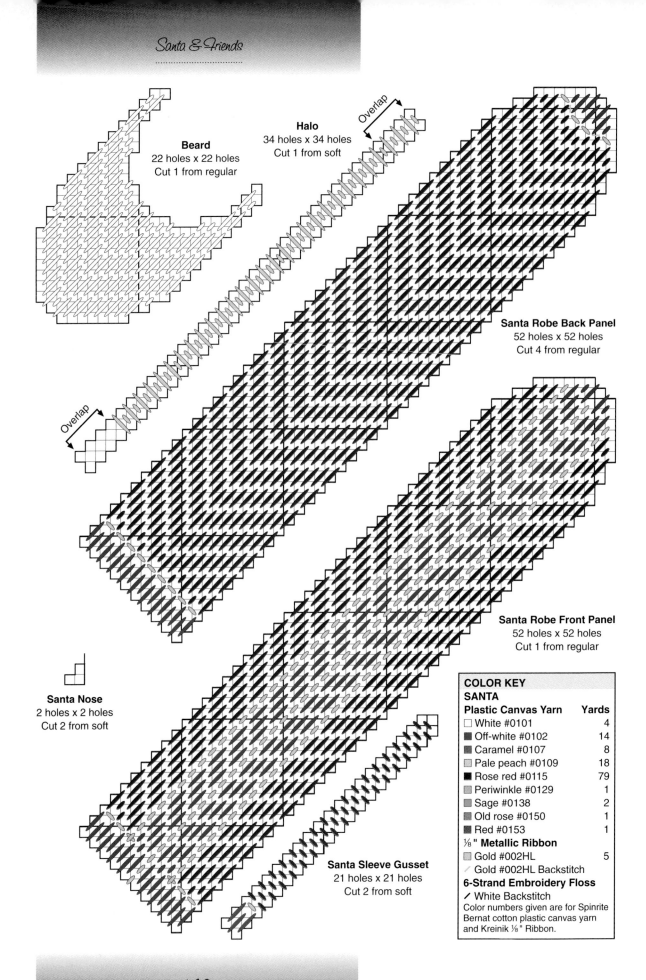

Beard
22 holes x 22 holes
Cut 1 from regular

Halo
34 holes x 34 holes
Cut 1 from soft

Overlap

Overlap

Santa Robe Back Panel
52 holes x 52 holes
Cut 4 from regular

Santa Robe Front Panel
52 holes x 52 holes
Cut 1 from regular

Santa Nose
2 holes x 2 holes
Cut 2 from soft

Santa Sleeve Gusset
21 holes x 21 holes
Cut 2 from soft

COLOR KEY
SANTA

Plastic Canvas Yarn	Yards
□ White #0101	4
■ Off-white #0102	14
■ Caramel #0107	8
▨ Pale peach #0109	18
■ Rose red #0115	79
▨ Periwinkle #0129	1
▨ Sage #0138	2
▨ Old rose #0150	1
■ Red #0153	1
⅛" Metallic Ribbon	
▨ Gold #002HL	5
╱ Gold #002HL Backstitch	
6-Strand Embroidery Floss	
╱ White Backstitch	

Color numbers given are for Spinrite Bernat cotton plastic canvas yarn and Kreinik ⅛" Ribbon.

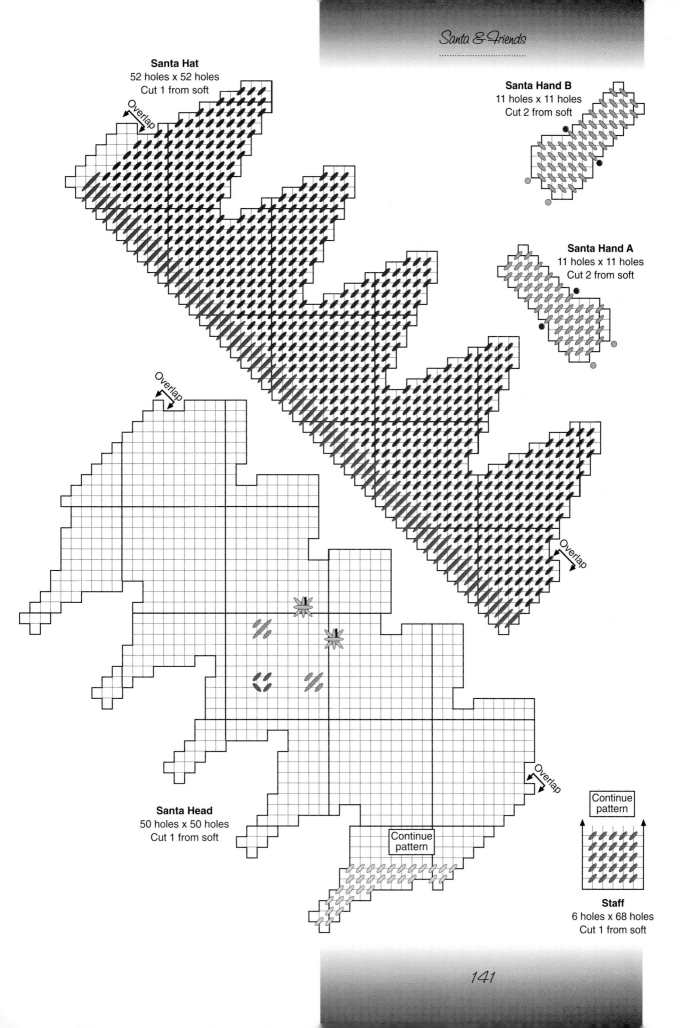

Santa Hat
52 holes x 52 holes
Cut 1 from soft

Overlap

Overlap

Santa Hand B
11 holes x 11 holes
Cut 2 from soft

Santa Hand A
11 holes x 11 holes
Cut 2 from soft

Overlap

Overlap

Continue
pattern

Santa Head
50 holes x 50 holes
Cut 1 from soft

Continue
pattern

Continue
pattern

Staff
6 holes x 68 holes
Cut 1 from soft

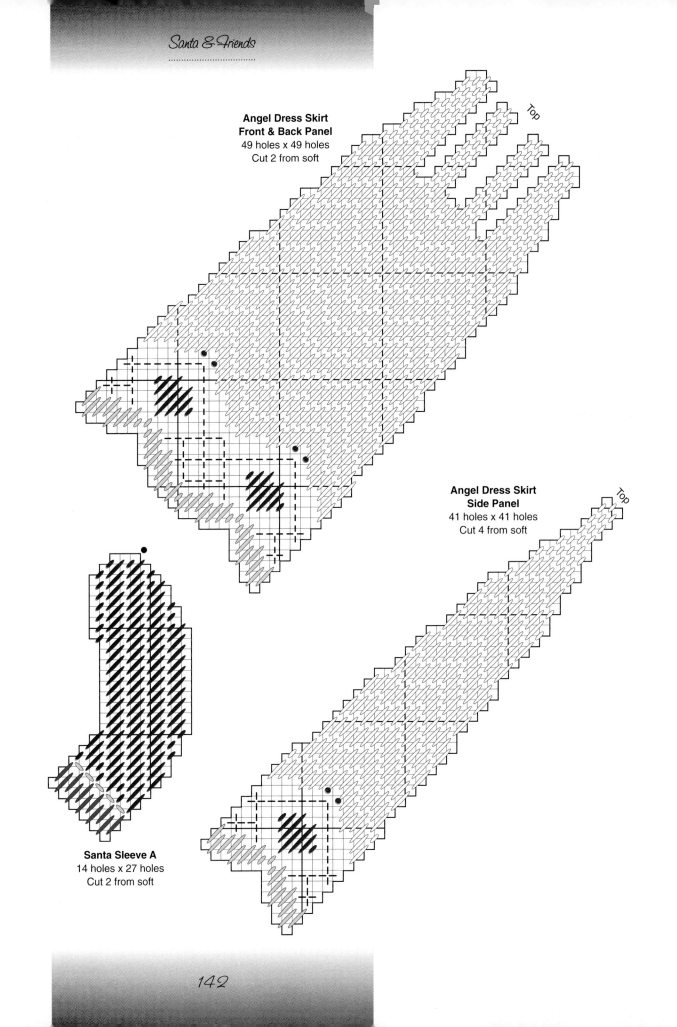

**Angel Dress Skirt
Front & Back Panel**
49 holes x 49 holes
Cut 2 from soft

TOP

**Angel Dress Skirt
Side Panel**
41 holes x 41 holes
Cut 4 from soft

TOP

Santa Sleeve A
14 holes x 27 holes
Cut 2 from soft

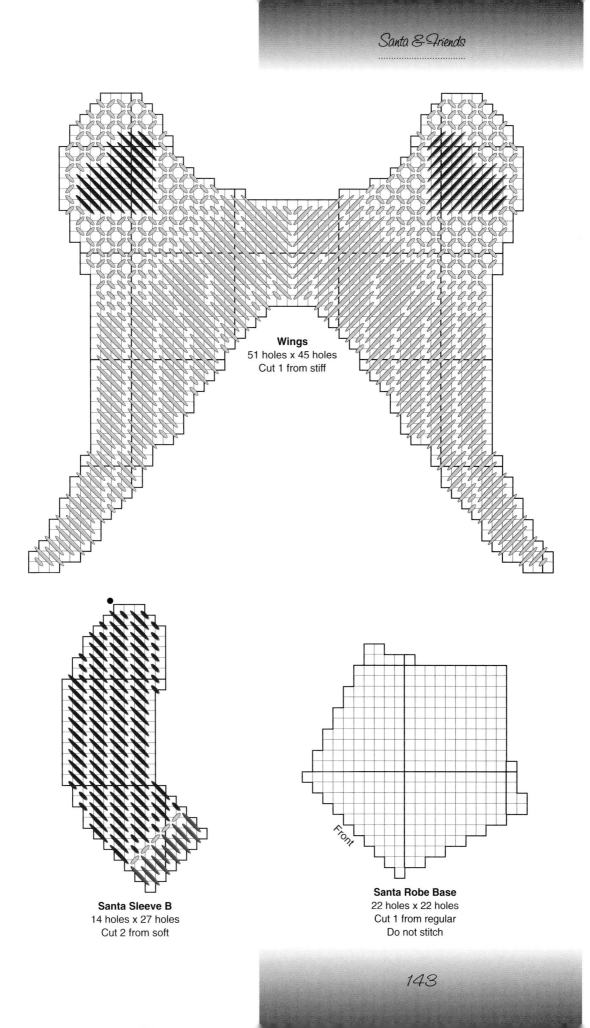

Wings
51 holes x 45 holes
Cut 1 from stiff

Santa Sleeve B
14 holes x 27 holes
Cut 2 from soft

Front

Santa Robe Base
22 holes x 22 holes
Cut 1 from regular
Do not stitch

Yo-yo Santa

This delightful Santa makes a terrific gift for a friend who enjoys crafting!

Skill Level: Advanced beginner

Materials

- 2 sheets 7-count plastic canvas
- Plastic canvas yarn as listed in color key
- #16 tapestry needle
- 15 small cream fabric yo-yos #7381
- 7½" white doll stand

Instructions

1. Cut plastic canvas according to graph.

2. Stitch front only following graph. Back will remain un-stitched. Add embroidery over completed background stitching.

3. Overcast bottom edge of front with natural. Whipstitch front and back together around sides and top with natural at hem, beard, face, pompon and sleeve and cap cuffs; scarlet at remainder of cap and sleeve edges; and brisk green at mittens and coat.

4. Using photo as a guide, glue one yo-yo to cap pompon and 14 yo-yos to beard, making two rows of four pompons at top of beard and two rows of three yo-yos at bottom.

5. Remove ring insert from top of doll stand and discard. Insert doll stand in opening at bottom of Santa.

— Designed by Joan Green

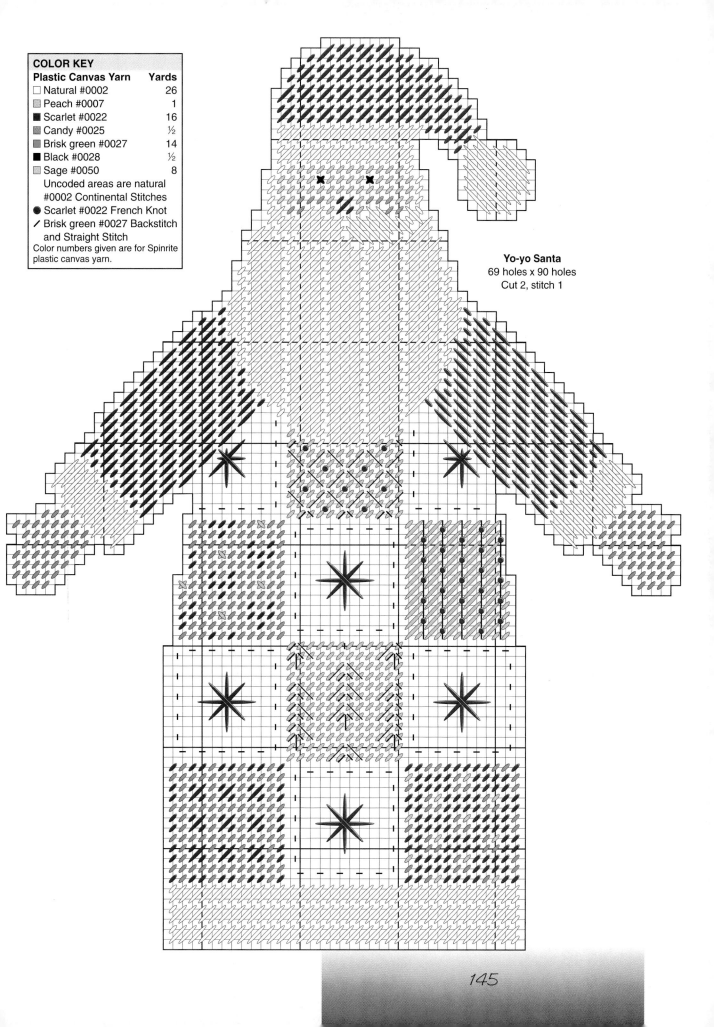

COLOR KEY

Plastic Canvas Yarn	Yards
☐ Natural #0002	26
☐ Peach #0007	1
■ Scarlet #0022	16
☐ Candy #0025	½
■ Brisk green #0027	14
■ Black #0028	½
☐ Sage #0050	8

Uncoded areas are natural
#0002 Continental Stitches

● Scarlet #0022 French Knot

╱ Brisk green #0027 Backstitch
and Straight Stitch

Color numbers given are for Spinrite
plastic canvas yarn.

Yo-yo Santa
69 holes x 90 holes
Cut 2, stitch 1

Jingle Santa

Liven up a wall or door with this cheerful Santa wall hanging! It's easy to stitch!

Skill Level: Beginner

Materials
- ⅔ sheet 7-count plastic canvas
- Plastic canvas yarn as listed in color key
- Plastic canvas metallic cord as listed in color key
- #3 pearl cotton as listed in color key
- 1⅓ yards 1⅜"-wide Christmas plaid ribbon
- 4 large gold jingle bells
- Hot-glue gun

Instructions

1. Cut plastic canvas according to graph.

2. Stitch piece following graph. Add French Knots over completed background stitching. Overcast with adjacent colors.

3. Fold ribbon in half. With red pearl cotton, sew one jingle bell through both halves approximately 5" from bottom of ribbon. Repeat with remaining three bells, going up ribbon and sewing in a row through both thicknesses approximately 1⅝" apart. Cut ribbon ends at an angle.

4. Cut a 2" length of red pearl cotton. Thread through fold at top of ribbon. Tie ends in a knot on inside of fold for hanging.

5. Glue Santa to ribbon front between top of ribbon and bells.

— Designed by Michele Wilcox

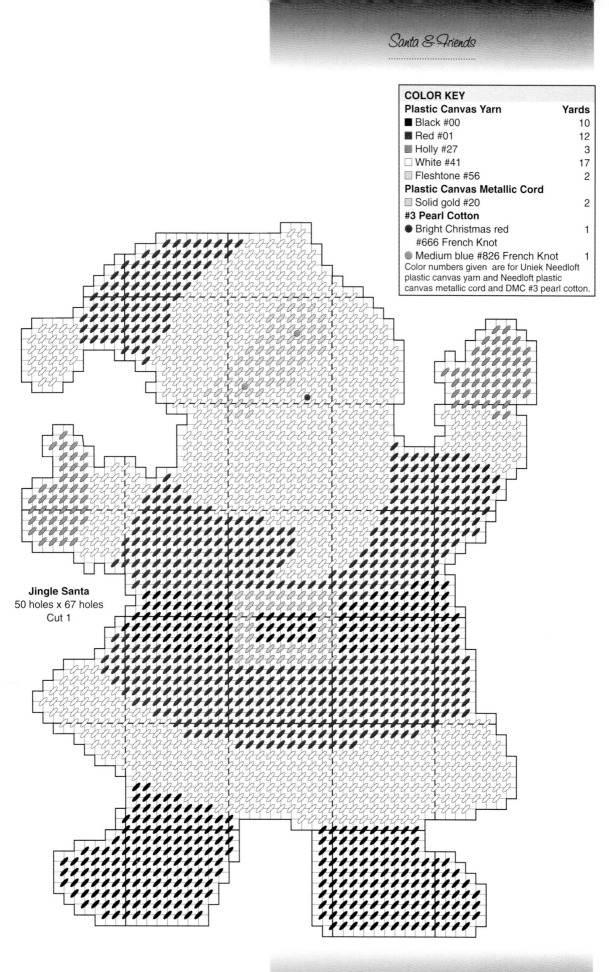

COLOR KEY

Plastic Canvas Yarn	Yards
■ Black #00	10
■ Red #01	12
■ Holly #27	3
□ White #41	17
☐ Fleshtone #56	2

Plastic Canvas Metallic Cord

☐ Solid gold #20	2

#3 Pearl Cotton

● Bright Christmas red #666 French Knot	1
● Medium blue #826 French Knot	1

Color numbers given are for Uniek Needloft plastic canvas yarn and Needloft plastic canvas metallic cord and DMC #3 pearl cotton.

Jingle Santa
50 holes x 67 holes
Cut 1

Mr. & Mrs. Snowman

Celebrate winter by crafting these two sweet snow people to display on a table or mantel!

Skill Level: Beginner

Materials

- 1 sheet 7-count plastic canvas
- Worsted weight yarn as listed in color key
- #16 tapestry needle
- 2 (3½") white doll stands

Instructions

1. Cut plastic canvas according to graphs.

2. Stitch fronts only following graphs. Backs will remain unstitched.

3. Backstitch over vest with 4 plies dark rose. Use 2 plies yarn for black and light green Backstitching.

4. Using 2 plies yarn and wrapping yarn around needle once, work French Knots for mouth on Mr. Snowman and eyes, nose and bow centers on Mrs. Snowman; wrap yarn around needle twice for Mr. Snowman's French Knot eyes.

5. With white, Overcast bottom edges of front pieces. Whipstitch Mr. Snowman front and back together around sides and top with black around hat and with white at remaining edges. Repeat with Mrs. Snowman, Whipstitching around hat with dark rose.

6. Remove ring insert from top of each doll stand and discard. Insert doll stand in opening at bottom of snow people.

— Designed by Joan Green

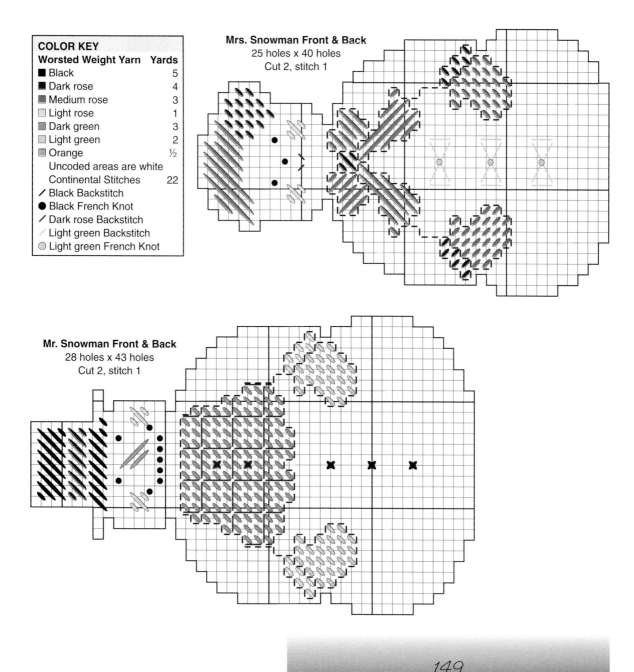

COLOR KEY

Worsted Weight Yarn	Yards
■ Black	5
■ Dark rose	4
▦ Medium rose	3
□ Light rose	1
▨ Dark green	3
□ Light green	2
▨ Orange	½
Uncoded areas are white Continental Stitches	22
╱ Black Backstitch	
● Black French Knot	
╱ Dark rose Backstitch	
╱ Light green Backstitch	
○ Light green French Knot	

Mrs. Snowman Front & Back
25 holes x 40 holes
Cut 2, stitch 1

Mr. Snowman Front & Back
28 holes x 43 holes
Cut 2, stitch 1

Santa Candy Cane Door Hanger

With just a few quick stitches and simple finishing touches, you can add this clever Christmas door decoration to any room in your home!

Skill Level: Beginner

Materials
- ¼ sheet 7-count stiff plastic canvas
- Plastic canvas yarn as listed in color key
- Plastic canvas metallic yarn as listed in color key
- #16 tapestry needle
- ½" red pompon
- 3 (⅜") gold jingle bells
- 2 white cotton terry chenille stems
- White sewing thread or embroidery floss
- Hot-glue gun

Instructions

1. Cut candy cane from plastic canvas according to graph.

2. Stitch piece following graph. Overcast with adjacent colors.

3. Cut chenille stems in half. *Note: Only three of the four lengths will be used in this project.* Wrap each of the three lengths around a pencil, forming a coil.

4. Glue coils in three vertical rows over stitched beard area (see photo). Glue pompon over stitched nose on face.

5. With white sewing thread or floss, sew three jingle bells to end of cap where indicated on graph.

— Designed by Joan Green

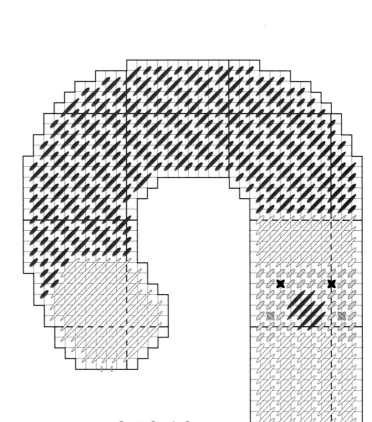

Santa Candy Cane
33 holes x 65 holes
Cut 1

COLOR KEY	
Plastic Canvas Yarn	**Yards**
☐ White #0001	6
☐ Peach #0007	1
■ Scarlet #0022	12
☐ Candy #0025	½
■ Black #0028	1
Plastic Canvas Metallic Yarn	
☐ Gold	½
ǀ Attach jingle bells	
Color numbers given are for Spinrite plastic canvas yarn.	

Angelina

With her sweet face and adorable curly hair, this little darling will delight your holiday guests, one and all!

Skill Level: Intermediate

Materials
- 1 sheet 7-count plastic canvas
- 2 (3") plastic canvas circles
- Plastic canvas yarn as listed in color key
- Pearlized metallic cord as listed in color key
- 7 yards bright metallic cord: gold #3411-01
- 6-strand embroidery floss as listed in color key
- 2 (11mm) movable eyes
- 2 (½") light pink pompons
- Strawberry blond curly doll hair
- 1"-tall basket
- 3 (½") red roses
- 3 small artificial leaves
- Polyester fiberfill
- Tacky craft glue
- Hot-glue gun

Cutting & Stitching

1. Cut plastic canvas according to graphs (page 153 and 155).

2. Stitch pieces following graphs, reversing two wings and one arm before stitching. Backstitch with 6 strands floss over completed Continental Stitching. Bottom piece will remain unstitched.

3. Overcast arms with adjacent colors. Matching edges, Whipstitch wrong sides of two wings together with white cord. Repeat with remaining two wings.

4. For halo, cut the five innermost rows of holes on each plastic canvas circle, leaving the four outermost rows of holes.

5. With gold cord, Straight Stitch each circle from the outside row of holes to innermost row of holes, working two stitches per hole in every other hole.

6. With gold cord, Whipstitch wrong sides of circles together around inside and outside edges.

Assembly

1. From green dot at top of head down the side to bottom edge, Whipstitch side A of angel front to side A of angel back with colors indicated on graphs; Whipstitch remaining edges of sides A together with adjacent colors. Repeat with sides B of angel front and back.

2. Stuff doll with fiberfill, then Whipstitch sides C of back pieces together from green dot at top of head to bottom edge with adjacent colors. With Christmas green, Whipstitch bottom piece to bottom edges of front and back pieces.

3. Using photo as a guide, glue one pompon to each end of mouth. Glue movable eyes side-by-side above cheeks.

4. Cut curly hair into desired lengths. Beginning at neck and working to top of head, use tacky glue to glue hair to head in layered rows over pumpkin stitches.

5. Apply a line of glue with glue gun along one outside edge of front piece between blue dots; matching arm edges to glue line, glue arm in place. Repeat with other arm on opposite side of front piece.

6. Hot-glue leaves and flowers inside basket; back of basket to doll below hands; and tip of hands to basket handle.

7. Hot-glue wings to doll where indicated on graph. Glue halo to head using photo as a guide.

— Designed by Nancy Marshall

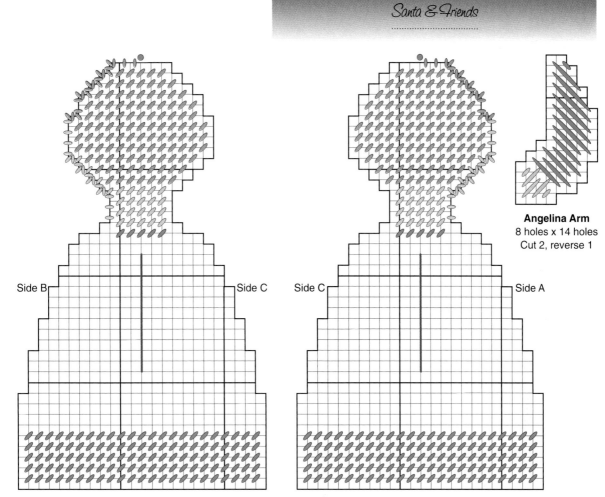

Angelina Backs
24 holes x 40 holes
Cut 1 each

Angelina Arm
8 holes x 14 holes
Cut 2, reverse 1

Angelina graphs continued on page 155

COLOR KEY

Plastic Canvas Yarn	Yards
▢ Peach #46	3½
▨ Pumpkin #50	5
▨ Christmas green #58	10
Uncoded areas are white #01	
Continental Stitches	15
Pearlized Metallic Cord	
▢ White #3410-01	10
6-Strand Embroidery Floss	
╱ Christmas red #321 Backstitch	½
❙ Attach wing to back	

Color numbers given are for Darice plastic canvas yarn and Bright Pearls metallic cord and DMC 6-strand embroidery floss.

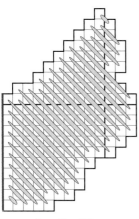

Angelina Wing
13 holes x 19 holes
Cut 4, reverse 2

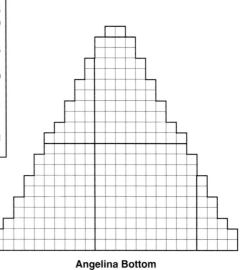

Angelina Bottom
24 holes x 21 holes
Cut 1, do not stitch

Happy Snowman Mug

This whimsical mug insert featuring one very happy snowman makes a great gift for someone who loves winter!

COLOR KEY

#3 Pearl Cotton	Yards
☐ White	8
◼ Black #310	2
▨ Light steel gray #318	1
◼ Dark pewter gray #413	1
☐ Very dark Christmas red #498	1
◼ Bright Christmas red #666	2
▨ Medium pink #818	1
▨ Christmas green #909	1
▨ Medium emerald green #911	1
▨ Pumpkin #971	1
Uncoded area is light blue #813 Continental Stitch	27

Color numbers given are for DMC #3 pearl cotton.

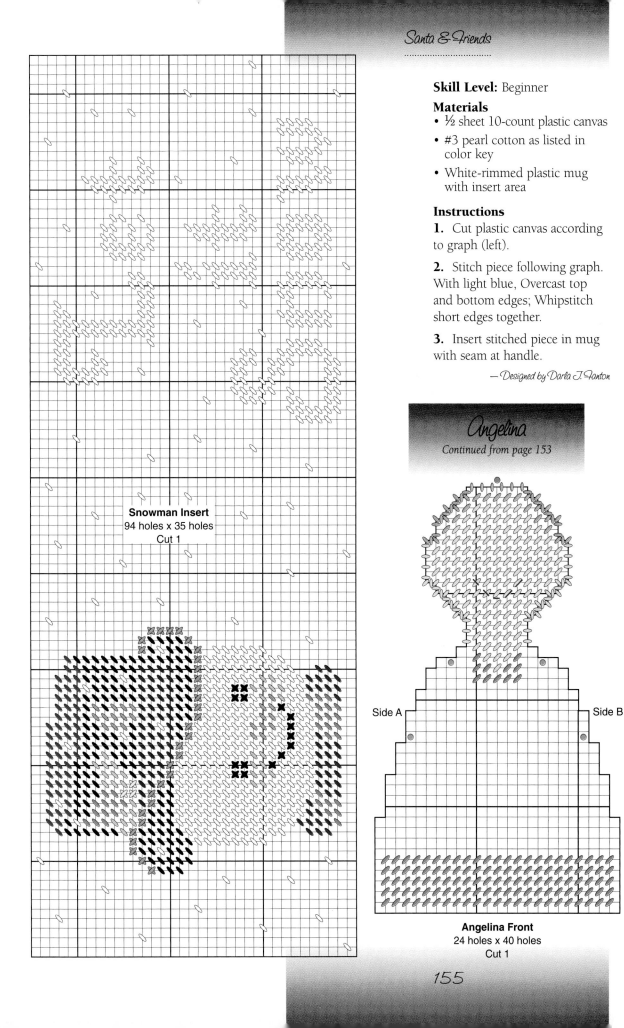

Skill Level: Beginner

Materials

- ½ sheet 10-count plastic canvas
- #3 pearl cotton as listed in color key
- White-rimmed plastic mug with insert area

Instructions

1. Cut plastic canvas according to graph (left).

2. Stitch piece following graph. With light blue, Overcast top and bottom edges; Whipstitch short edges together.

3. Insert stitched piece in mug with seam at handle.

—Designed by Darla J. Fanton

Angelina
Continued from page 153

Snowman Insert
94 holes x 35 holes
Cut 1

Side A   Side B

Angelina Front
24 holes x 40 holes
Cut 1

Stitch Key

Use the following diagrams to expand your plastic canvas stitching skills. For each diagram, bring needle up through canvas at the red number one and go back down through the canvas at the red number two. The second stitch is numbered in green. Always bring needle up through the canvas at odd numbers and take it back down through the canvas at the even numbers.

Background Stitches

The following stitches are used for filling in large areas of canvas. The Continental Stitch is the most commonly used stitch. Other stitches, such as the Condensed Mosaic and Scotch Stitch, fill in large areas of canvas more quickly than the Continental Stitch because their stitches cover a larger area of canvas.

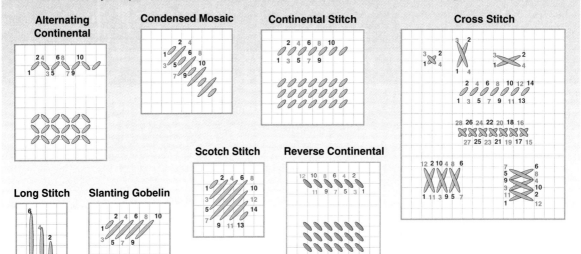

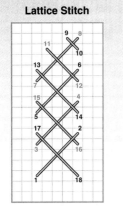

Embroidery Stitches

Embroidery stitches are worked on top of a stitched area to add detail and beauty to your project. Embroidery stitches are usually worked with one strand of yarn, several strands of pearl cotton or several strands of embroidery floss.

Lattice Stitch

Chain Stitch

Straight Stitch

Fly Stitch

Couching
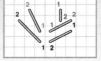

Back Stitch
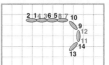

Embroidery Stitches

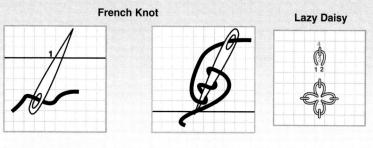

French Knot

Lazy Daisy

Bring yarn needle up through canvas, then back down in same hole, leaving a small loop.

Then, bring needle up inside loop; take needle back down through piece on other side of loop.

Bring needle up through piece.

Wrap yarn around needle 2 or 3 times, depending on desired size of knot; take needle back through piece through same hole.

Specialty Stitches

The following stitches can be worked either on top of a previously stitched area or directly onto the canvas. Like the embroidery stitches, these too add wonderful detail and give your stitching additional interest and texture.

Diamond Eyelet

Smyrna Cross

Satin Stitch

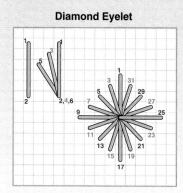

For each stitch, bring needle up at odd numbers around outside and take needle down through canvas at center hole.

This stitch gives a "padded" look to your work.

Finishing Stitches

Both of these stitches are used to finish the outer edges of the canvas. Overcasting is done to finish one edge at a time. Whipstitch is used to stitch two pieces of canvas together. For both Overcasting and Whipstitching, work one stitch in each hole along straight edges and inside corners, and two or three stitches in outside corners.

Overcast Whipstitch

Loop Stitch or Turkey Loop Stitch

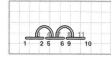

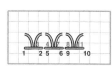

The top diagram shows this stitch left in tact. This is an effective stitch for giving a project dimensional hair. The bottom diagram demonstrates the cut loop stitch. Because each stitch is anchored, cutting it will not cause the stitches to come out. A group of cut loop stitches give a fluffy, soft look and feel to your project.

Acknowledgments

We'd like to thank the following manufacturers who have generously provided our designers with materials and supplies. We appreciate their contribution to the production of this book.

The Beadery Craft Products
P.O. Box 178
Hope Valley, RI 02832
(401) 539-2432
- Beads—Candy Cane Huggers, Country Angel
- Cabochons—Candy Cane Huggers
- Faceted stones—Folk-Art Santa & Angel (Angel)

Coats & Clark
Craft & Yarn Division
30 Patewood Dr.
Greenville, SC 29615
(803) 234-0331
- Anchor 6-strand embroidery floss—Ice Crystals
- J. & P. Coats Acrylic Craft Yarn Art. E.48—NOEL Quartet, Ribbons & Bows Frame, Peppermint Candy
- J. & P. Coats plastic canvas yarn—Folk-Art Icicle Santas, Folk-Art Stripe Stocking, Father Christmas
- Red Heart Classic yarn—Let It Snow!, Christmas Canister Covers, Poinsettia Coasters, Quick & Easy Gifts (Snowman Plant Poke)

Creative Beginnings
475 Morro Bay Blvd.
Morro Bay, CA 93442
(805) 772-9030
- Brass charms—Country Angel

Daniel Enterprises
P.O. Box 1105
Laurinburg, NC 28353
(910) 277-7441
- Crafter's Pride Stitch-A-Mug™—Happy Snowman Mug

Darice mail order:
Bolek's Craft Supplys Inc.
P.O. Box 465
330 N. Tuscarawas Ave.
Dover, OH 44622-0465
(216) 364-8878
- Bright Jewels Cord—Winter Welcome Wreath, Angelina
- Bright Pearls Cord—Winter Welcome Wreath, Folk-Art Santa & Angel (Angel), Angelina
- Clock movement—German Christmas Clock
- Jingle bells—Surprise Bear, Snowman Match Holder
- Metallic cord—Winter Welcome Wreath
- Movable eyes—Surprise Bear, Snowman Match Holder
- Nylon Plus™ plastic canvas yarn—Nutcracker Caddy, Winter Welcome Wreath, Angelina
- Plastic canvas—Surprise Bear, Candy Cane Huggers, Folk-Art Icicle Santas, Christmas

Memories (Green Album), Fleur-de-lis Mantel Scarf, Nutcracker Caddy, Winter Welcome Wreath, Merry Christmas, Mr. & Mrs. Santa Bear, Poinsettia Coasters, Country Angel, Holly & Chickadee, Striped Star Candy Dish, Festive Christmas Jewelry (Gingerbread Barrette, Jingle Bell Pull Pin, Topiary Tree Pin, Stocking Earrings), Quick & Easy Gifts (Snowman Plant Poke, Candy Canes Magnet), Folk-Art Stripe Stocking, Gifts for the Bookworm (Potted Poinsettia Bookmark, Berry Best Friends, Friends Are Dear to the Heart), Folk-Art Santa & Angel (Santa), Happy Snowman Mug, Angelina
- Plastic canvas heart—Angel Wings
- Straw satin raffia—Miniature Display Tree
- Super Soft™ plastic canvas—Christmas Canister Covers, Victorian Patchwork, Folk-Art Santa & Angel (Santa, Angel)
- Ultra Stiff plastic canvas—Swiss Tudor Cottages, Christmas Memories (White Album), German Christmas Clock, Miniature Display Tree, Let It Snow!, Snowman Match Holder, Christmas Canister Covers, Folk-Art Santa & Angel (Angel), Santa Candy Cane Door Hanger

The DMC Corp.
10 Port Kearny
South Kearny, NJ 07032
(201) 589-0606
- #3 pearl cotton—Surprise Bear, Merry Christmas, Santa's Workshop, Festive Christmas Jewelry (Gingerbread Barrette, Topiary Tree Pin), Gifts for the Bookworm (Potted Poinsettia Bookmark), Happy Snowman Mug, Jingle Santa
- #5 pearl cotton—Swiss Tudor Cottages, Christmas Memories (Green Album), Santa's Workshop, Festive Christmas Jewelry (Jingle Bell Pull Pin)
- 6-strand embroidery floss—Christmas Sparkle Ornaments, Angel Wings, Fleur-de-lis Mantel Scarf, Santa Claus Coasters, Holly & Chickadee, Gifts for the Bookworm (Berry Best Friend, Friends Are Dear to the Heart), Angelina

Fairfield Processing Corp.
88 Rose Hill Ave.
P.O. Drawer 1157
Danbury, CT 06810
(203) 744-2090
- Poly-Pellets®—Handy Stocking Holders

Fibre-Craft Materials Corp.
6310 W. Touhy Ave.
Niles, IL 60714
(708) 647-1140

- Doll stand—Mr. & Mrs. Snowman, Yo-yo Santa
- Cotton terry chenille stems—Santa Candy Cane Door Hanger

Fond Memories
One Terminal Way
Norwich, CT 06360
(203) 887-4789
- Acrylic Hang-Up (HU01)—Holiday Home Accents
- Designer acrylic switch plate (SPP02)—Holiday Home Accents

Kreinik Mfg. Co. Inc.
3106 Timanus Ln.
Baltimore, MD 21244
(410) 281-0040
- ⅛" Ribbon—Angel Wings, Peppermint Candy, Elegant Desk Accessories, Folk-Art Santa & Angel (Santa, Angel)
- 1/16" Ribbon—Christmas Sparkle Ornaments, Festive Christmas Jewelry (Stocking Earrings), Ice Crystals
- Fine (#8) Braid—Festive Christmas Jewelry (Stocking Earrings)
- Medium (#16) Braid—Ice Crystals
- Heavy (#32) Braid—Victorian Patchwork, Father Christmas

Kunin Felt Co./Foss Mfg. Co. Inc.
380 Lafayette Rd.
P.O. Box 5000
Hampton, NH 03842
(800) 292-7900
- Felt—Festive Christmas Jewelry (Stocking Earrings)

Lion Brand Yarn Co.
34 W. 15th St.
New York, NY 10011
(212) 243-8995
- Lion Chenille—Victorian Patchwork

Madeira Marketing Ltd.
600 E. Ninth St.
Michigan City, IN 46360
(219) 873-1000
- GlissenGloss™ Braid Ribbon Four™—Striped Star Candy Dish
- GlissenGloss™ Estaz™—Festive Christmas Jewelry (Stocking Earrings)

Mangelsen's
9706 Mockingbird Dr.
Omaha, NE 68127
(402) 339-3922
- Metallic craft cord—Beary Special Christmas

Mill Hill/Gay Bowles Sales, Inc.
P.O. Box 1060
Janesville, WI 53547
(608) 754-9466

- Ceramic buttons—NOEL Quartet, Gingerbread House, Gifts for the Bookworm (Berry Best Friend, Friends Are Dear to the Heart)
- Seed beads— Elegant Desk Accessories

One & Only Creations
P.O. Box 2730
Napa, CA 94558
(800) 262–6768
- Curly doll hair—Folk-Art Santa & Angel (Santa, Angel), Angelina

Rainbow Gallery mail order:
Designs by Joan Green
6345 Fairfield Rd.
Oxford, OH 45056
(513) 523–2690
- Fyreworks™ metallic ribbon—Festive Christmas Jewelry (Jingle Bell Pull Pin)
- Gold Rush—Christmas Remembered, Miniature Display Tree
- Plastic Canvas 7 Metallic Yarn—Jolly St. Nick, German Christmas Clock, Fleur-de-lis Mantel Scarf, Christmas Canister Covers

Rhode Island Textile Co.
P.O. Box 999
Pawtucket, RI 02862
(401) 722–3700
- RibbonFloss™—Christmas Memories (White Album), Holiday Home Accents, Quick & Easy Gifts (Festive Sachets, Mom & Dad Key Rings), Gifts for the Bookworm (Friends Are Dear to the Heart)

- Metallic RibbonFloss™—Holiday Home Accents, Quick & Easy Gifts (Festive Sachets, Mom & Dad Key Rings)

St. Louis Trimming, Inc.
5040 Arsenal St.
St. Louis, MO 63139
(314) 771–8388
- Floral print ribbon—Elegant Desk Accessories
- Mylar cord—Elegant Desk Accessories

Shafaii Co.
1000 Broadway
Houston, TX 77012
(713) 923–5300
- Cystals—Folk-Art Santa & Angel (Santa)
- Fabric yo-yos—Yo-yo Santa

Spinrite, Inc.
Box 40
Listowel, Ont., N4W 3H3
- Berella "4" worsted weight yarn—Gingerbread House
- Bouquet Christmas Sparkle yarn—Fleur-de-lis Mantel Scarf
- Plastic canvas yarn—Candy Cane Huggers, Festive Jinglers, Christmas Memories (Green & White Albums), German Christmas Clock, Miniature Display Tree, Fleur-de-lis Mantel Scarf, Snowman Match Holder, Gingerbread House, Striped Star Candy Dish, Santa Candy Cane Door Hanger, Yo-yo Santa
- Bernat plastic canvas cotton yarn—Folk-Art

Santa & Angel (Santa, Angel)

Uniek Inc.
P.O. Box 457
805 Uniek Dr.
Waunakee, WI 53597
(608) 849–9999
- Needloft® plastic canvas cord—Mr. & Mrs. Santa Bear, Country Angel, Jingle Santa
- Needloft® plastic canvas yarn—Beary Special Christmas, Country Christmas Charm, Swiss Tudor Cottages, Merry Christmas, Country Button Tree, Mr. & Mrs. Santa Bear, Country Angel, Mini Stocking Ornament, Quick & Easy Gifts (Candy Canes Magnet), Jingle Santa
- Plastic canvas star—Striped Star Candy Dish
- Quick-Count™ plastic canvas—Holiday Home Accents, Quick & Easy Gifts (Festive Sachets, Mom & Dad Key Rings)

Wang's International
4250 Shelby Dr.
Memphis, TN 38118
(901) 375–3085
- Flocked Santa bear—Beary Special Christmas, Santa's Workshop, Mini Stocking Ornament
- Flocked half-bear—Beary Special Christmas

Westrim Crafts
9667 Canoga Ave.
P.O. Box 3879
Chatsworth, CA 91313
(818) 998–8550
- Fun Foam—Poinsettia Coasters

Special Thanks

Angie Arickx
Beary Special Christmas, Swiss Tudor Cottages, Mr. & Mrs. Santa Bear, Mini Stocking Ornament

**Martha Bleidner &
Celia Lange of Celia Lange Designs**
Surprise Bear, Christmas Memories (Green Album), Miniature Display Tree, German Christmas Clock, Fleur-de-lis Mantel Scarf, Let It Snow!, Snowman Match Holder, Christmas Canister Covers, Poinsettia Coasters, Gifts for the Bookworm (Potted Poinsettia Bookmark), Quick & Easy Gifts (Snowman Plant Poke)

Mary Cosgrove
Holiday Home Accents, Quick & Easy Gifts (Festive Sachets, Mom & Day Key Rings)

Phyllis Dobbs
Nutcracker Caddy,
Santa Claus Coasters

Darla Fanton
Candy Cane Huggers, Christmas Memories (White Album), Folk-Art Santa & Angel, Happy Snowman Mug

Joan Green
Festive Jinglers, Angel Wings, Gingerbread House, Victorian Patchwork, Mr. & Mrs. Snowman, Santa Candy Cane Door Hanger, Yo-yo Santa

Habegger Furniture
Berne, IN for the use of the hutch shown on page 134.

Judi Kauffman
NOEL Quartet, Christmas Sparkle Ornaments, Ribbons & Bows Frame, Peppermint Candy, Festive Christmas Jewelry (Stocking Earrings), Ice Crystals

Kathleen Kennebeck
Quick & Easy Gifts (Candy Canes Magnet)

Carol Krob
Elegant Desk Accessories

Nancy Marshall
Folk-Art Icicle Santas, Folk-Art Stripe Stocking, Angelina

Karen McDanel
Handy Stocking Holders

Adele Mogavero
Country Angel

Trudy Bath Smith
Winter Welcome Wreath

Alyssa VanHorn
Shown on page 7, from the Charmaine Model Agency, Fort Wayne, IN

Karen Wiant
Holly & Chickadee

Michele Wilcox
Country Christmas Charm, Country Button Tree, Merry Christmas, Jingle Santa

Lois Winston
Father Christmas

Kathy Wirth
Striped Star Candy Dish

Linda Wyszynski
Gifts for the Bookworm (Berry Best Friend, Friends Are Dear to the Heart)